Games to Play with Babies

Third Edition

Jackie Silberg

Illustrated by Laura D'Argo

Jackie Silberg

Games to Play with Babies

NEW REVISED! 50 New Games!

Viva Books

New Delhi | Mumbai | Chennai | Kolkata | Bangalore | Hyderabad | Kochi

Third Edition

Dedication

This book is dedicated to the joy that babies bring into our lives.

Acknowledgements

Thanks to Kathy Charner, the most wonderful editor an author can have.
She makes the words come alive.
And to the Gryphon House family who work together to produce the beautiful product that you are looking at now.

First Indian Edition 2004
Reprinted 2005, 2008

VIVA BOOKS PRIVATE LIMITED

- 4737/23 Ansari Road, Daryaganj, New Delhi 110 002
  E-mail: vivadelhi@vivagroupindia.net, Tel. 42242200
- Plot No. 76, Service Industries, Shirvane, Sector 1, Nerul, Navi Mumbai 400 706,
  E-mail: vivamumbai@vivagroupindia.net, Tel. 27721273, 27721274
- Jamals Fazal Chambers, 26 Greams Road, Chennai 600 006
  E-mail: vivachennai@vivagroupindia.net, Tel. 28290304, 28294241
- B-103, Jindal Towers, 21/1A/3 Darga Road, Kolkata 700 017
  E-mail: vivakolkata@vivagroupindia.net, Tel. 22836381, 22816713
- 7, Sovereign Park Apartments, 56-58, K. R. Road, Basavanagudi, Bangalore 560 004
  E-mail: vivabangalore@vivagroupindia.net, Tel. 26607409, 26607410
- 101-102 Mughal Marc Apartments, 3-4-637 to 641, Narayanguda, Hyderabad 500 029
  E-mail: vivahyderabad@vivagroupindia.net, Tel. 27564481, 27564482
- First Floor, Beevi Towers, SRM Road, Kaloor, Kochi 682 018, Kerala
  E-mail: vivakochi@vivagroupindia.net, Tel: 0484-2403055, 2403056

Published by arrangement with

Gryphon House, Inc.
10726 Tucker Street
Beltsville, Maryland MD 20705
USA

The publisher and the author cannot be held responsible for injury, mishap, or damages incurred during the use of or because of the activities in this book. The author recommmends appropriate and reasonable supervision at all times based on the age and capability of each child.

ISBN-10: 81-7649-854-8
ISBN-13: 978-81-7649-854-8

Published by Vinod Vasishtha for Viva Books Private Limited, 4737/23, Ansari Road, New Delhi 110 002. Printed and bound by Raj Press, R-3, Inderpuri, New Delhi - 110 012.

Table of Contents

From the Author 9
Guidelines for Growth 11

Games for 0-3 months

Tender Touching 17
Sweet Dreams 18
Good Night, Baby 19
Good Night Kisses 20
Sleepy Time 21
Loving Kisses 22
Touching Time 23
Special Times 24
Coos and Hugs 25
Stroke the Baby 26
Baby Boop 27
Tickle Cheek 28
Texture Glove 29
Playing With Fingers 30
Dance a Merry Jig 31
Baby's Fingers 32
Rattles and Teethers 33
Baby's Bath 34
Grass Games 35
I See You 36
Baby Aerobics 37
'Round the Mountain 38
Exercise Fun 39
Kick, Kick, Kick 40
Turn Over, Baby 41
No Distractions 42
Find the Noise 43
High and Low 44
Squeaky Toys 45
Listen to the Sounds 46
Different Voices 47
Follow the Bee 48
Tongue Fun 49
Mouth Noises 50
Bedtime Talk 51
Moving the Sound 52
Learning With Classics 53
A Language Game 54
Can You Find Me? 55
Black and White 56
Seeing the World 57
The Umbrella Mobile 58
Birdie, Birdie, Tweet, Tweet 59
Mirror Fun 60
What Can I Look At? 61
Hold It Tight 62
The Hand Discovery 63
Oh, How Pretty 64
Moving the Picture 65
The Tracking Game 66
Flashlight Tracking 67
Puppet Games 68

Games for 3–6 months

Sleepy Time 71
Hush-a-Bye 72
Swim Little Fishie 73
What's Cooking? 74
All Around the House 75
The Stroking Game 76
Reaching 77
Exploring 78
Bumping Noses 79
Baby's Fingers 80
Hello, Hands 81
Fascinating Toes 82
This Little Toe 83
Fingers and Toes 84
Five Little Fingers 85
Touch Your Fingers 86
This Little Piggy 87
Where Is Thumbkin? 88
Kick Those Legs 89
The Rolling Surprise 90
Up and Down the Elevator 91
Bouncy, Bouncy 92
Fly, Baby, Fly 93
Diaper Fun 94
The Spider Game 95
Here Comes a Bug 96
Cockle Doodle Doo 97
Here's the Spoon! 98
Hand Fun 99
Jelly in the Bowl 100
Baby's Bottle 101
Reach Out and Touch 102
How Does It Feel? 103
Tapping Away 104
Rhythm Talk 105
Shake, Shake, Shake 106
Where's the Sound? 107
Silly Sounds 108
Sing, Sing, Sing 109
Twinkle, Twinkle 110
Talk to Me, Baby 111
Talking to Your Baby 112
The Name Game 113
The Body Game 114
Talk, Talk, Talk 115
Look, Look, Look 116
Remembering 117
Roly-Poly Books 118

Games for 6-9 months

Relieving Stress 121
A New Peek-a-boo 122
The Napkin Game 123
Which Hand Is It? 124
Backstroke Baby 125
Who Do You See? 126
Zip, Zip, Zip 127
Rattle, Rattle, Rattle, Rattle, Bing! 128
Where's Your Toe? 129

Pinkety Pinkety 130
Creeping 131
Little Mouse 132
Circles and Music 133
Baby Massage 134
Where's the Mousie? 135
Stretch Up High 136
One, Two, Kick! 137
Ball Rolls 138
Bend and Stretch 139
The Dropping Game 140
Crawling Fun 141
Floor Games 142
Tug of War 143
The Floating Game 144
The Exploring Game 145
Three Blocks, Two Hands 146
What Toy Is It? 147
Cup Games 148
The Cracker Game 149
The Macaroni Game 150
Muffin Tin Game 151
The Spoon Game 152
Pots and Pans 153
Fast-Food Fun 154
The Dancing Game 155
The Paper Game 156
Feels Good 157
Touch This 158
Texture Crawl 159
What Happens Next 160
Where's the Doll? 161
Sound vs. Silence 162
Familiar Sounds 163
Choo, Choo, Choo, Happy Game 164
Mama, Dada 165
Name the Clothes 166
Using Signs with Words 167
The Baby Story 168
Telephone Talk 169
Loo Loo Loo 170
Bang It and Shake It 171
Making Music 172
Music Listening 173
Old MacDonald 174
Song Cues 175
One, Two, One, Two 176

Games for 9–12 months

Sleep Song 179
Niño Querido 180
Newcastle Lullaby 181
Sleep Story 182
I See the Moon 183
Shoe Game 184
Combing Game 185
Powder Puff Fun 186
The Rainmaker 187
The Washing Game 188
A Bath Surprise 189
Squeeze Fun 190
Floating Surprise 191
Catch the Toy 192

Let's Find Daddy 193
Shopping Fun 194
It's Cold 195
Left, Right, Cross the Street 196
Wrapping with Babies 197
Make a Toy 198
Mr. Bear 199
Object Hide-and-Seek 200
Where Did It Go? 201
Give Me the Toy 202
Ribbon Fun 203
Gathering Treasures 204
Crackers 205
I Can Do It Myself 206
Look, I Can Pour! 207
Water and Spoon 208
Find the Snack 209
Choo, Choo, Food 210
Counting Buttons 211
Does It Fit? 212
Boxes, Boxes 213
Stack Them Up 214
Drop the Clothespin 215
Find the Bell 216
Hats, Hats, Hats 217
Drawing in the Snow 218
Tap and Clap 219
Through the Hole 220
Whoops, Johnny 221
So-o-o Big 222
Mirror Parts 223
Open, Shut Them 224
Copy Me 225
Tunnel Fun 226
Let's Play Ball 227
The Toy Chase 228
In the Sky 229
Mommy Tunnel 230
High Steps 231
The Feely-Touchy Game 232
M-m-m Nice 233
The Bye-bye Game 234
The Banana Game 235
The Shoebox Game 236
The Glove Game 237
Two Tube Games 238
Upside Down Game 239
Sticky Game 240
The Cardboard Game 241
Trampoline Game 242
The Elbow Game 243
Pushing Game 244
Singing Fun 245
Where's the Music? 246
Speech Rhythms 247
Wee Willie Winkie 248
Huff and Puff 249
Where's the Foot? 250
Simple Directions 251
Special Book 252

Index 253

From the Author

For as long as I can remember, I have loved spending time with young children. There is something so joyous in a baby's smile and laughter. For the past twenty years, I have taught classes for parents and babies together. We share times filled with songs, movement, games, fun, and learning. The parents have shared with me games that they play with their babies. All of the games in this book have been played and enjoyed by babies.

Playing games with babies is a valuable learning experience for babies and a bonding experience for both adult and child. Healthy bonding and attachment to loving caregivers give babies the emotional security so essential to their total development.

The latest brain research affirms the importance of stimulating babies to help their brain cells form connections, paving the way for future learning. The games in this book will help to "grow" the connections in babies' brains. In addition, they will improve babies' listening and language skills, spark their curiosity, increase their awareness of their bodies, and help them develop a sense of humor. Each game describes what babies will learn by playing it.

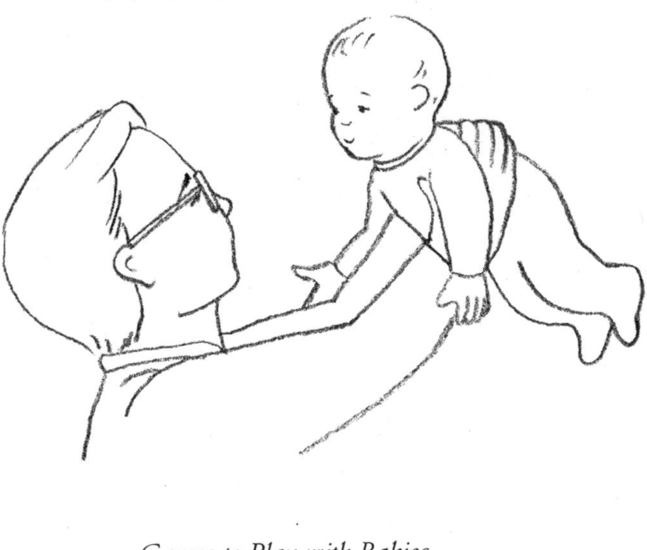

Observe babies closely as they interact with their environment and play these games. By responding to their interests and abilities, you are creating a healthy and challenging environment that will promote babies' physical, mental, social, and emotional growth. Also remember that babies need time alone. Sometimes they don't want to be picked up or played with. With your loving time, patience, and warmth, all the games in this book will give babies a beautiful beginning in life. Play these games with babies. Hold them close to you. Cuddle, pat, touch, kiss, and enjoy every single moment!

Jackie Silberg

Age range

The age range given for each activity is an approximation. Remember that each child develops at his or her own pace. Use your knowledge of each individual child as the best judgment as to whether an activity is appropriate.

Guidelines for Growth

Birth to Six Months

Motor, auditory, and visual skills
Holds up her head
Grasps a rattle or a toy
Rolls from her back to her side
Sits with hand support
Pulls to a sitting position while holding an adult's finger
Follows moving objects with his eyes
Focuses her eyes on small objects
Begins to reach for objects
Picks up blocks
Transfers objects from hand to hand
Reacts with a start to loud noises
Turns his head in the direction of a bell
Turns her head toward the sound of a voice
Responds to a voice with activity

Language and cognitive skills
Babbles and coos
Gurgles upon seeing others
Makes simple sounds like "ahhh" and "oooh"
Says one sound repeatedly
Smiles, giggles, and laughs
Attempts to make a variety of sounds
Makes sounds when attended to
Smiles in response to attention
Shows eagerness by making sounds
Fusses when a favorite toy is removed
Responds differently to handling
Reacts to the sight of a toy

Shows awareness of a change in routine
Attempts to repeat motions
Reacts to strangers

Self-concept skills
Inspects her own hands
Brings things to his mouth
Focuses her eyes on her moving hands
Smiles at a mirror image
Makes sounds to mirror images
Anticipates feeding time
Plays unattended for ten minutes or more
Picks up a spoon
Feeds himself crackers
Holds a bottle part of the time
Lifts a cup with a handle
Looks directly at a person's face
Recognizes parents and other familiar people
Reaches for familiar people
Responds to "peek-a-boo"
Smiles in response to facial expressions

Six to Twelve Months

Motor, auditory, and visual skills
Bounces up and down in a standing position
Sits unsupported
Pulls pegs from a pegboard
Rolls a ball while sitting
Crawls rapidly
Climbs on stairs
Stands unaided
Moves her hand to follow what her eyes focus upon
Picks up small objects with his thumb and finger
Puts a few blocks in a cup
Bangs two blocks together

Looks at pictures in a book
Drops small objects into containers
Responds to tones and inflections in voices
Recognizes familiar words and responds accordingly
Shakes a bell in imitation
Stops an activity after hearing "no"
Shows interest in certain words and gestures

Language and cognitive skills
Imitates speech sounds
Babbles rhythmically
Combines two syllables like "Dada" or "Mama"
Imitates the sounds of animals
Says the first real words other than "Mama" and "Dada"
Attracts attention by making noises
Imitates clapping hands
Waves "bye-bye"
Follows simple directions
Understands "no"
Shakes head to indicate "no"
Pulls strings to obtain a toy
Finds a block hidden under a cup
Knows the meaning of "Dada" and "Mama"
Removes a block from a cup when shown how
Squeezes toys to make a squeak
Looks to find toys no longer in sight

Self-concept skills
Seeks or demands attention
Pushes away another's hands to keep a toy
Holds her arms in front of her face to avoid being washed
Holds his arms out to be picked up
Sucks on soft foods from a spoon
Holds, bites, and chews a cracker or a biscuit
Feeds herself with her fingers
Drinks from a cup with help

Controls drooling
Responds to gestures
Plays and enjoys "patty cake"
Repeats a performance when laughed at
Encourages an audience
Cooperates in dressing by holding out his arms

0–3 months

WHAT YOUR BABY WILL LEARN:
Developing Trust

Tender Touching

- One way infants learn about relationships is by the way they are touched and held. Gentle touching at this tender age helps develop their sense of trust.
- Hold your baby close to you and speak softly as you tell her how much you love her.
- Gently stroke her face as you say loving words to her.
- Always include her name in the words that you speak. This provides her with an identity that is important.
- Whenever you hold your baby and speak to her, keep the same tone of voice. Soon she will know that your voice means good things.

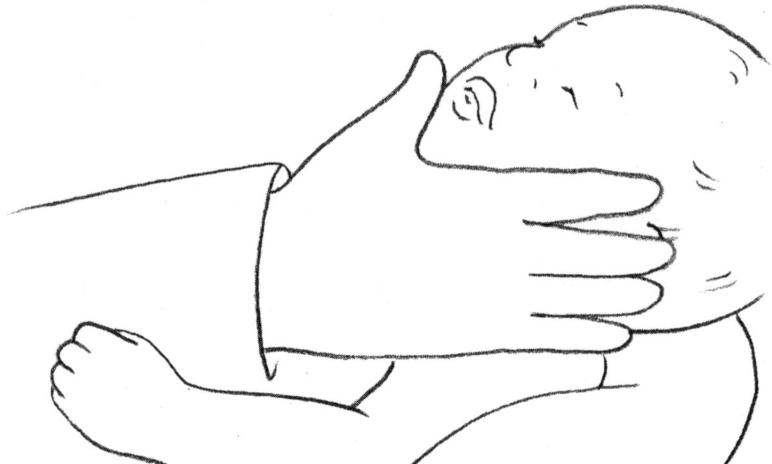

0-3 months

WHAT YOUR BABY WILL LEARN:
Bonding

Sweet Dreams

- Infants often move about looking for something to suck or cuddle as they try to quiet themselves and relax for sleep.
- Help the process along and make it easier for the baby to fall asleep.
- Put a soft stuffed animal (one that is safe for infants) or a blanket into the crib.
- Take your baby's hand and put it on the toy or blanket.
- Say, "Good night, baby, sweet dreams, baby" in a soft voice.
- Soon your baby will know that when she feels that toy or blanket, she will be comforted.

0–3 months

WHAT YOUR BABY WILL LEARN:
Bonding

Good Night, Baby

- While your baby is nursing or drinking a bottle, gently massage her fingers and toes.
- Softly sing songs such as "Twinkle, Twinkle, Little Star."
- Keep repeating this song as you massage the baby's fingers and toes.
- This game will help the baby associate feeding with your loving touch.
- Singing to babies while they are nursing or drinking a bottle is pleasurable for both you and your baby.

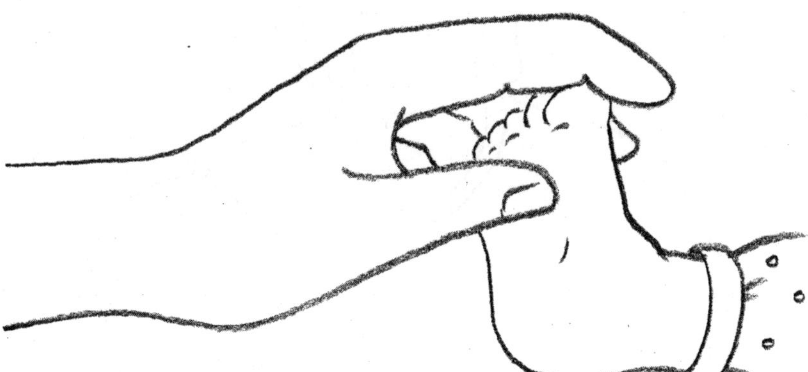

0–3 months

WHAT YOUR BABY WILL LEARN:
Bonding

Good Night Kisses

- Rock your baby gently in your arms.
- Dim the light in the room so it is soft and muted.
- Kiss the baby on the forehead and say:

  I love you, I love you,
  I love my little (child's name).

- Kiss the baby on her fingers and repeat the words.
- Continue kissing the baby on different parts of her body as you repeat the words.

WHAT YOUR BABY WILL LEARN:
Trust

Sleepy Time

- Caring tenderly for babies makes them feel loved and accepted.
- Singing lullabies while swaying with the baby in your arms is a wonderful way to develop trust.
- Some traditional lullabies that you can sing are:

    Hush Little Baby
    Rock-a-bye Baby
    All the Pretty Horses
    Hush-a-bye

- Think of lullabies. Sing or say them to your baby as you rock her and hold her close.

WHAT YOUR BABY WILL LEARN:
Body Awareness

Loving Kisses

- This game is lovely to play as you dress the baby or change her diaper.
- Say, "I love your nose, nose, nose, nose." Kiss the baby on her nose.
- Say, "I love your tummy, tummy, tummy." Kiss the baby on her tummy.
- Name other parts of her body and kiss them.
- This game helps the baby become aware of her body and of the love that you express.

WHAT YOUR BABY WILL LEARN:
Bonding

Touching Time

- When your baby is nursing or drinking a bottle, it is important to hold and cuddle her.
- The baby's arms and hands should be free to let her touch and explore as she feeds.
- Place your baby's hands on your face. Move her hands across your nose, mouth, hair, and eyes.
- Hold her hands and gently massage them.
- Stroke her arms and speak softly to her.

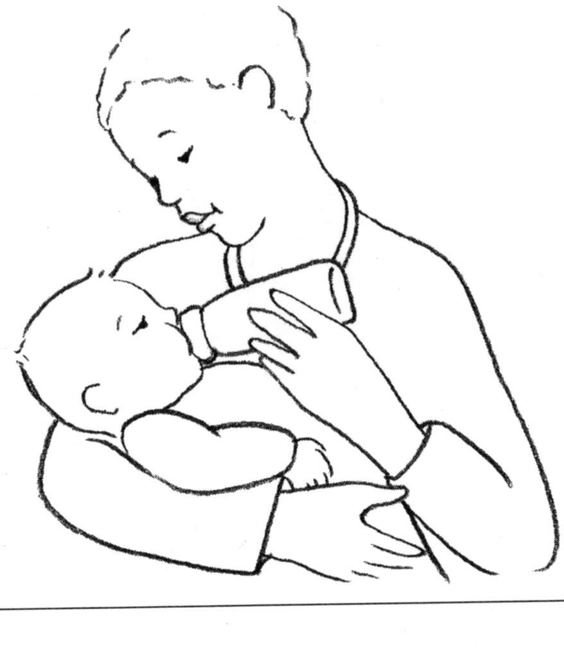

0–3 months

WHAT YOUR BABY WILL LEARN:
Trust

Special Times

- Newborns respond to touching and sounds. Each time you pick up your baby and speak to her, you are establishing trust between the two of you.
- The tone of your voice and the strength of your arms will become familiar to your infant.
- Be consistent in the way you hold your baby, the things that you say to her, and the tone of your voice.
- Soon your baby will coo and smile at you. This is her way of communicating her love.

WHAT YOUR BABY WILL LEARN:
Language Skills

Coos and Hugs

- The language of infants is cooing. When an infant sees something of interest, she responds with a coo.
- Play a cooing game with your baby. Hold a brightly colored object in front of the baby's eyes. When the baby responds with a coo, answer her with a coo and a hug.
- You will soon find out what pleases your baby.
- When babies learn that their sounds please another person, they will make more sounds. This encourages early language development and talking.

WHAT YOUR BABY WILL LEARN:
Bonding

Stroke the Baby

- This is a wonderful bonding game that encourages loving interaction between the baby and the adult.
- Find a variety of objects with which to stroke your baby. A blanket, feather, cotton ball, or silk are all excellent choices.
- Hum softly as you stroke the baby. Lullabies are nice.
- Rub the baby's fingers and toes one at a time as you hum. The baby will enjoy this very much.
- Next stroke the baby's fingers and toes one at a time with each object.

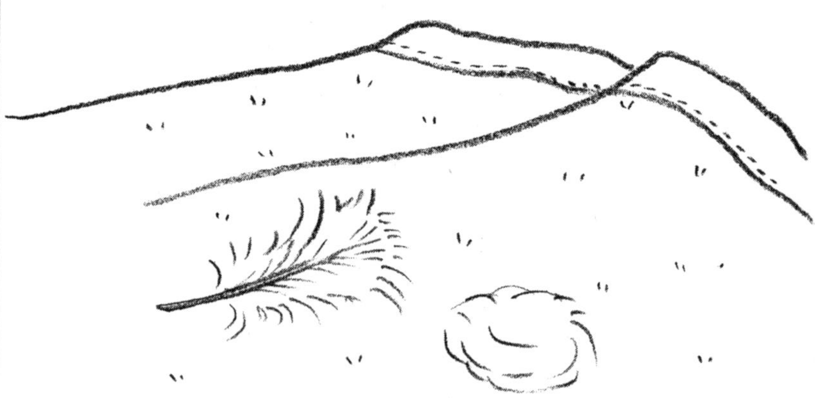

WHAT YOUR BABY WILL LEARN:
Social Skills

Baby Boop

- This is a good game to play while changing your baby's diaper.
- Lay the baby on her back. Touch the baby's body in different places and make the sound "boop" with each touch.
- Your baby may smile each time you touch her and visibly anticipate your next touch in a new place.
- When you make the "boop" sound, also name the part of the body you touch.

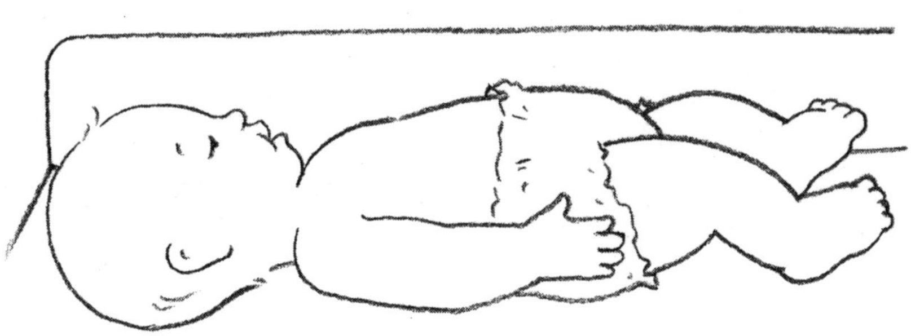

0–3 months

WHAT YOUR BABY WILL LEARN:
Fun

Tickle Cheek

- There is nothing more delightful than a smiling baby. This game will encourage your baby to smile a lot.
- Rock your baby back and forth in your arms very gently.
- Softly stroke the skin near her mouth with your index finger.
- When she smiles at you, praise her and let her know how pleased you are.
- Try this game. Stroke the baby's face three times, then say, "Smile." As you stroke her face, count to three. "One, two, three....smile."

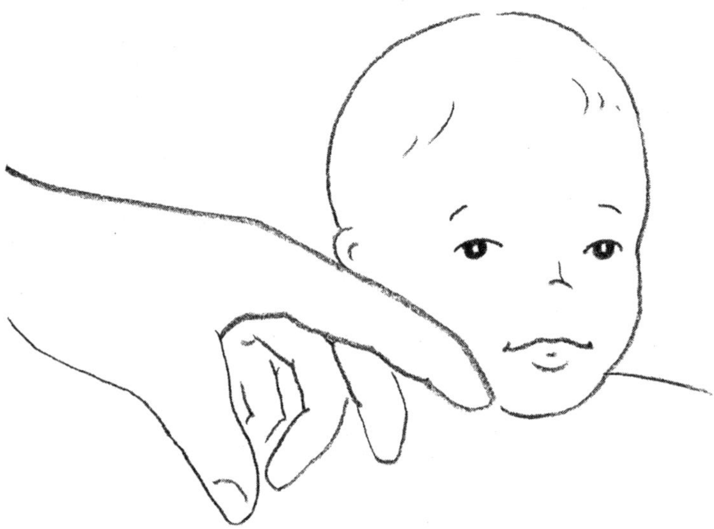

WHAT YOUR BABY WILL LEARN:
About Textures

Texture Glove

- Cover an old glove with different textured materials. ***NOTE***: Securely attach all materials.
- Secure a different fabric to each finger of the glove.
- Flannel, silk, velvet, and linen work well. Try attaching a large button or similar large object, also.
- If you cut the fingertips off the gloves, the baby can feel your fingernails as well as the textures of the fabrics.

0-3 months

WHAT YOUR BABY WILL LEARN:
About Body Parts

Playing With Fingers

- Watch your baby to see what she does with her fingers and plan games to help her practice these skills.
- If she is opening and closing her fingers, give her toys such as rattles to grasp.
- If she is wiggling her fingers, help her to wiggle them and praise her as you help.
- If she is touching parts of her body, say the name of that body part as she touches it.
- This is how babies learn.

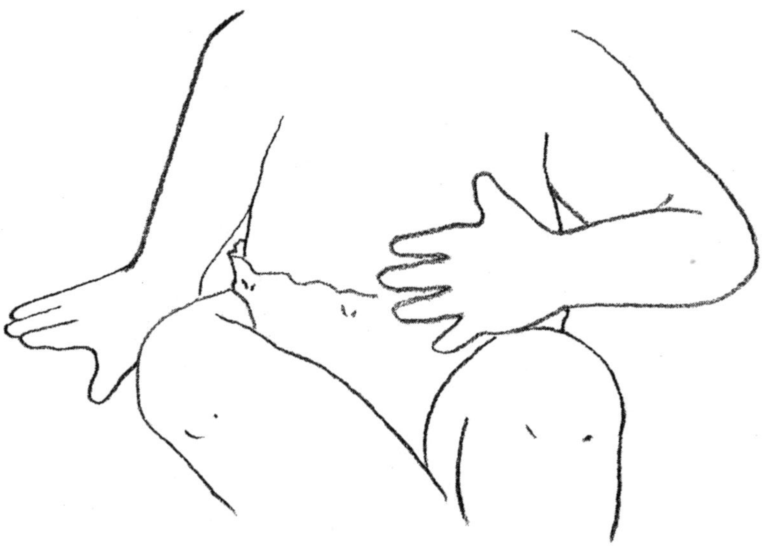

0–3 months

WHAT YOUR BABY WILL LEARN:
Body Awareness

Dance a Merry Jig

- Play this game with either your baby's fingers or toes. Alternating them makes your baby become more aware of her hands and feet.
- Touch one finger or toe at a time as you chant:

This little pig danced a merry, merry jig,
This little pig ate candy.
This little pig wore a blue and yellow wig,
This little pig was a dandy.
But this little pig never grew very big,
And they called her "itty bitty Mandy." (Use your child's name.)

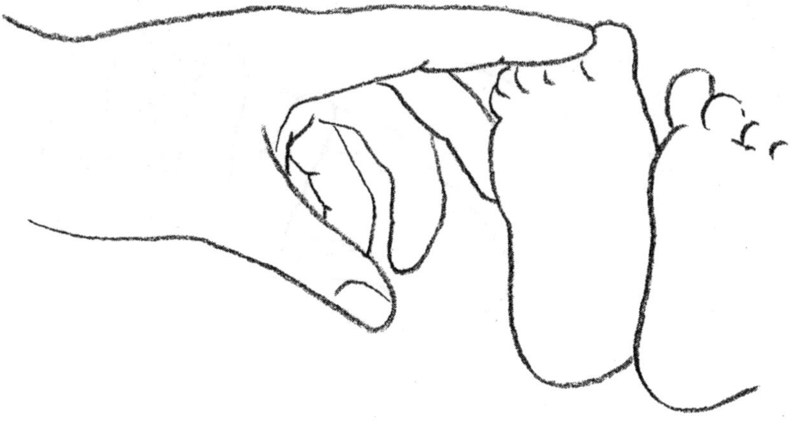

WHAT YOUR BABY WILL LEARN:
Body Awareness

Baby's Fingers

- This game involves lots of touching and helps babies begin to identify parts of their bodies.
- Touch the parts of the baby's body that are mentioned in the song as you name them.

Where, oh where, are baby's fingers?
Where, oh where, are baby's toes?
Where's the baby's belly button?
'Round and 'round it goes.
Where, oh where, are baby's ears?
Where, oh where, is baby's nose?
Where's the baby's bellybutton?
'Round and 'round it goes.

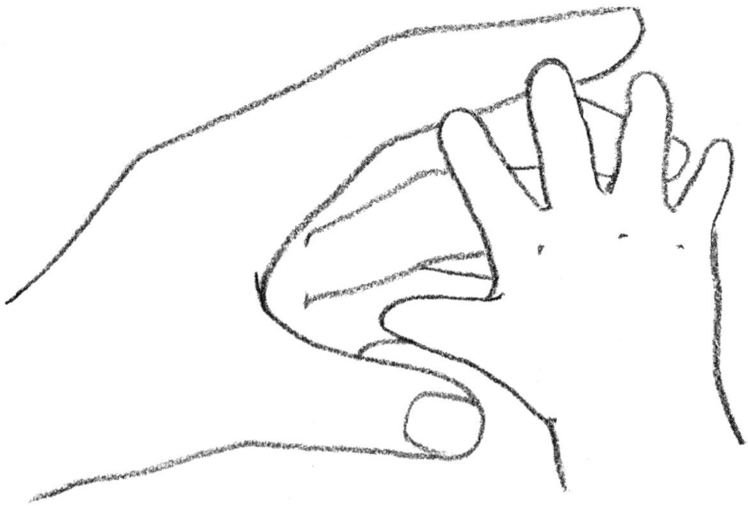

WHAT YOUR BABY WILL LEARN:
Coordination

Rattles and Teethers

- Play this game when the baby is alert. Put the baby in an infant seat.
- Place a rattle in the baby's hand. The baby may only hold the rattle for a few seconds and then drop it.
- Pick up the rattle and give it to the baby again.
- Soon the baby will bring the rattle to her mouth. At this stage of development, any object in a baby's hand becomes something for the mouth. You will know when it's time to add a teether.

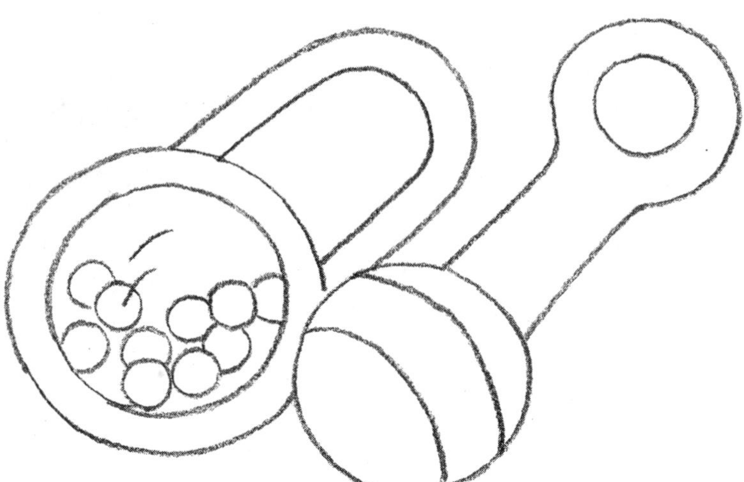

WHAT YOUR BABY WILL LEARN:
Bonding

Baby's Bath

- After the baby has learned to enjoy her bath, for a relaxing change of pace, take a warm bath with your baby.
- Hold the baby as you rock back and forth.
- Sing to the baby as you rock. Make up songs like, "We are taking a bath together," "I love my little baby, baby, baby," and so on.
- The song is not important, but the bonding is.

0–3 months

WHAT YOUR BABY WILL LEARN:
About Textures

Grass Games

- Go outside on a mild day. Spread a blanket on the ground and sit on it with your baby.
- Pick a blade of grass and gently stroke the baby on the arm with it.
- Turn the baby on her tummy and place the baby's hand on the grass. Move her hand back and forth across it.
- The baby will try to grasp the grass and find it very exciting.

0–3 months

WHAT YOUR BABY WILL LEARN:
To Lift Her Head

I See You

- Lie on your back and put your baby on your tummy. Call her name and raise her slightly to encourage her to lift her head to see you.
- Repeat this game over and over, praising the baby each time she lifts her head a little bit.
- Try the same game by putting the baby on the floor on her tummy. Hold a brightly colored object in front of her to encourage her to lift her head.
- Each time she lifts her head a little, praise her.

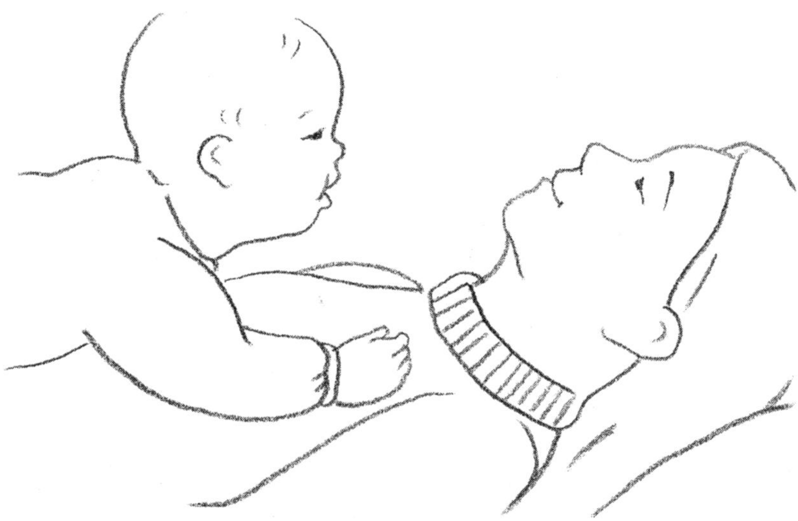

WHAT YOUR BABY WILL LEARN:
Exercise

Baby Aerobics

- Lay your baby on her back. Lift and lower her arms very gently.
- Cup her feet on the palms of your hands and move them in and out.
- Move her feet in a circle and then move her hands in a circle.

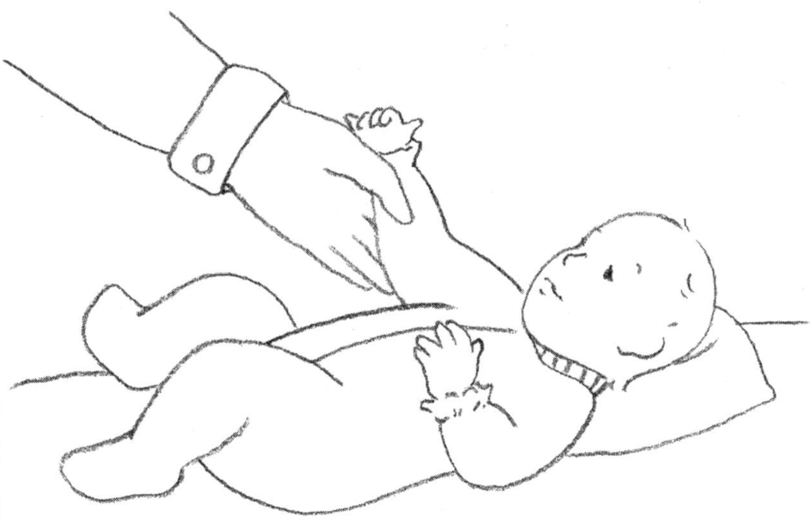

WHAT YOUR BABY WILL LEARN:
Body Awareness

'Round the Mountain

- It is important for your baby to exercise her legs.
- Lay your baby on her back and cup her feet on the palms of your hands.
- Move her legs in and out, then in a circle.
- As you move the baby's legs, sing the following song to the tune of "Go In and Out the Window."

Go 'round and 'round the mountain,
Go 'round and 'round the mountain,
Go 'round and 'round the mountain,
And kiss those little toes.

- On the last line, kiss each toe, one by one.

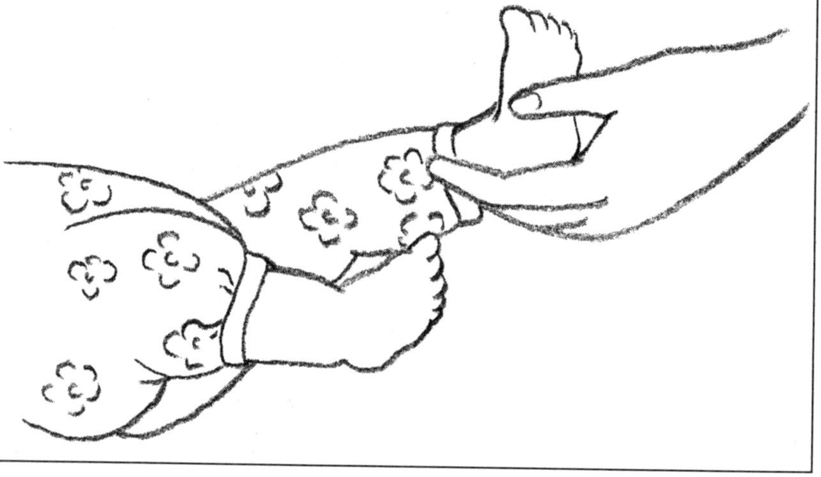

WHAT YOUR BABY WILL LEARN:
Exercise

Exercise Fun

- This game will tone your baby's muscles and help develop her sense of rhythm.
- Put your baby on her back and gently move her arms and legs to the rhythm of a nursery rhyme.
- Say the words to "Baa, Baa, Black Sheep" as you move her hands in a circle.
- Say the words to "Diddle, Diddle, Dumpling" as you move her legs back and forth.

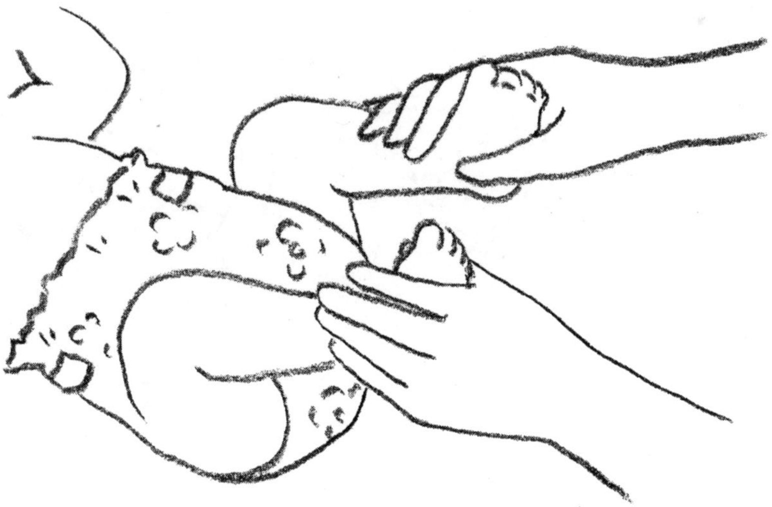

0–3 months

WHAT YOUR BABY WILL LEARN:
Exercise

Kick, Kick, Kick

- Babies enjoy kicking and lifting their legs. As you well know, babies put their toes into their mouths at a very young age.
- To help your baby practice kicking, place items at the baby's feet such as stuffed animals, squeaky toys, or your hand.
- Place one item at a time at your baby's feet.
- Hold a pillow at the baby's feet and let her kick it.

0–3 months

WHAT YOUR BABY WILL LEARN:
To Roll Over

Turn Over, Baby

- Babies become aware of their bodies through intentional movements. Turning over by herself is an intentional movement.
- Lay the baby on her back. Sit behind her head and hold a small toy above her face.
- When you are sure that you have the baby's attention, move the toy over to one side.
- Do this very slowly and encourage the baby to grab for the toy. If she turns over, give her the toy.
- Repeat the same activity on her other side.
- If the baby has part of her body turned and needs a little help, give her a gentle push.
- The more you play this game, the sooner the baby will realize that she can turn over by herself—an intentional movement.

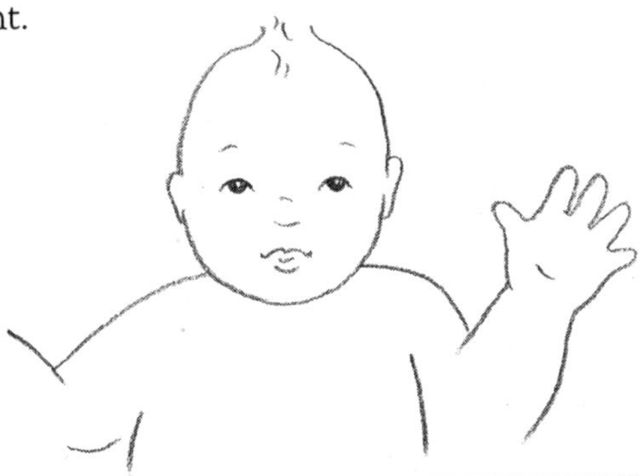

0-3 months

WHAT YOUR BABY WILL LEARN:
Calmness

No Distractions

- In the first months of a baby's life, maintaining a low level of stimulation is important. It reduces her stress and helps her to be more alert.
- Talk to your infant in a soft, slow voice.
- Turn off background noise such as the radio or television.
- Cuddle her in quiet places so that there are no distractions. Remember, she is adjusting from the noises in the womb to the noises in the world.
- Speak softly to her or sing the songs that you sang to her when she was in the womb.

WHAT YOUR BABY WILL LEARN:
About Sounds

Find the Noise

- After your baby has finished eating, hold her in your lap and play this game.
- Shake a rattle on one side of her head, then on the other side.
- Shake it slowly at first, then faster.
- Your baby will search for the noise with her eyes. When you see her responding to the sound, praise and cuddle her.

0–3 months

WHAT YOUR BABY WILL LEARN:
About Sounds

High and Low

- One of the newborn's most highly developed abilities is responding to sound, including the difference between high- and low-pitched sounds.
- Hold your baby close to you and say her name in a soft, high-pitched voice. For example, say, "Susie, Susie, I love you."
- Next, say the same words in a soft, low-pitched voice.
- Alternate between using high and low voices several times.

WHAT YOUR BABY WILL LEARN:
Body Awareness

Squeaky Toys

- Sit in a chair with your baby in your lap.
- Squeeze a squeaky toy.
- Place the toy in the baby's hand. She will grasp it as a natural reflex and will be surprised when it squeaks.
- Keep giving her the toy, and soon she will realize that it is her hand making the toy squeak.

WHAT YOUR BABY WILL LEARN:
About Sounds

Listen to the Sounds

- Sit the baby outside near a tree where she can watch the leaves move.
- Tie lightweight items to the branches so your baby can hear the sounds they make when they move in a breeze.
- Chimes, foil pie pans, and necklaces make lovely sounds as the wind blows through them.
- Talk about the sounds that the baby hears. Use words like "soft," "high," "tinkling," and any others you think of. The sounds will be peaceful to the baby.

WHAT YOUR BABY WILL LEARN:
Auditory Skills

Different Voices

- Your baby is starting to single out the different sound patterns of language.
- Talking to your baby in different voices will help her in the process.
- The more animated you make your voice, the more your baby will pay attention.
- Pick a short poem or song that you plan to teach your baby like "Twinkle, Twinkle Little Star" or "Mary had a Little Lamb."
- Sing or say the words in many different ways—low, high, softly, in a whisper, and in a happy voice.

WHAT YOUR BABY WILL LEARN:
Observation Skills

Follow the Bee

- Sit in a comfortable chair and hold your baby in your arms.
- Hold your finger in the air and make a buzzing sound.
- Move your finger around as you buzz.
- The baby's eyes will follow the "bee." Land the "bee" on the baby with a slight tickle.
- Repeat this many times.
- Now, hold the baby's finger in the air. Move her finger around the same way you moved your finger and land it on your cheek.
- Babies enjoy this very much.

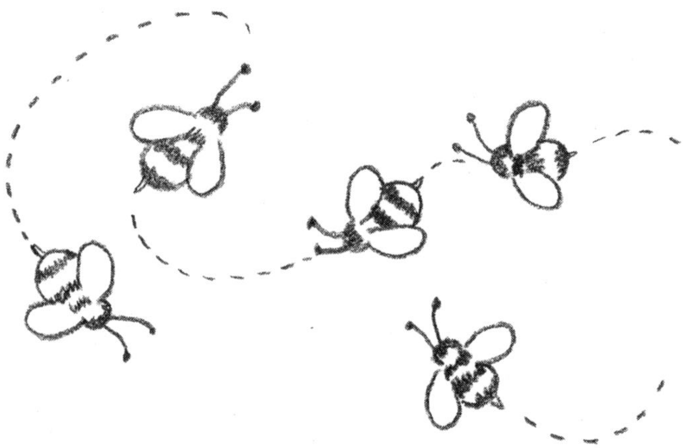

WHAT YOUR BABY WILL LEARN:
Imitation

Tongue Fun

- Infants will imitate the faces and sounds that you make.
- Hold the baby and get her attention.
- Stick out your tongue and make a noise at the same time.
- Your baby will try to imitate you by opening her mouth and sticking out her tongue, too.
- Try moving your tongue up and down or side to side, and see what your baby does!

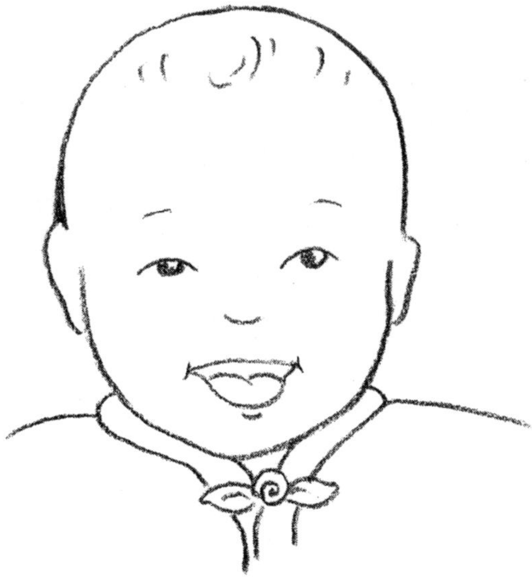

0–3 months

WHAT YOUR BABY WILL LEARN:
Language Skills

Mouth Noises

- Imitate the noises that your baby makes with her mouth. This will establish wonderful communication between you and your baby.
- Try some of the following suggestions:
- Kissing.
- Tongue clicking.
- The raspberry.
- A "ch ch" sound.
- Sticking your index finger in your mouth and popping it out.
- Blowing out and sucking in air.
- Making a "bub bub" sound by moving your lips up and down with your index finger while humming.

WHAT YOUR BABY WILL LEARN:
Language Skills

Bedtime Talk

- The more you talk to your baby, the sooner she will babble and try to talk.
- When it's bedtime, your soothing voice and loving words can help her fall asleep more easily.
- Say things like "Good night, sweet baby," or "Rest, rest, rest your little head."
- Hold the baby close to you and stroke her face or head as you talk to her.
- As you put her in her crib, continue to say comforting words as you caress her.

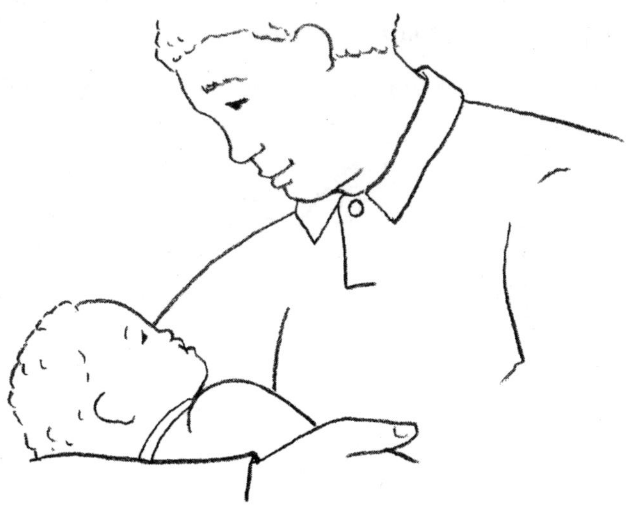

0-3 months

WHAT YOUR BABY WILL LEARN:
Listening Skills

Moving the Sound

- Make a concentrated effort to develop your baby's auditory skills. This is very valuable and will help her tune into sounds more easily.
- Lay your baby on the floor on her tummy.
- Lie down next to her and sing a little tune.
- She will move her head toward you. If she doesn't move her head, then gently move it for her.
- Now move to the other side of your baby and do the same thing.
- Continue playing this game in different places. For example, try it while sitting on a chair with the baby in your lap or during diaper changes.
- In addition to your voice, you can use rattles and bells to make the sounds.

WHAT YOUR BABY WILL LEARN:
Music Appreciation

Learning With Classics

- Listening to classical music with your baby is a wonderful way to bond with her and encourage her brain development for math and spatial reasoning.
- Play instrumental music (Mozart is suggested) as you hold your baby and rock to the music.
- Stroke her head and her back and put her face next to yours.
- Turn off the music and whisper loving words into her ear.
- Turn on the music again and continue stroking her head and back.

WHAT YOUR BABY WILL LEARN:
Language Skills

A Language Game

- An infant's brain will respond to every sound produced in any language. This is the perfect age to introduce sounds from another language.
- This game is just for fun.
- Pick a word like "hello" and learn to say it in a different language.
- Each day, greet your baby with "hello" in English or "hola," which is Spanish for "hello." This is just an example—you can choose any language.
- Select single words that relate to what your baby does each day. Say the English word and then the foreign word.
- Start with everyday words or phrases, such as "drink," "eat," "I love you," or various body parts and animals.

WHAT YOUR BABY WILL LEARN:
About Sounds

Can You Find Me?

- This game is good practice for coordinating sound and sight.
- While the baby is in her crib, go to another part of the room and call her name.
- Go back to where she is and say her name as you stroke her head.
- Go to another part of the room and say the baby's name.
- Then return to her and repeat her name as you stroke her head.
- As you continue to say her name in different parts of the room, the baby will move her eyes in search of the sound. By returning to the crib each time, you ensure that she hears the sound close by as well as far away.

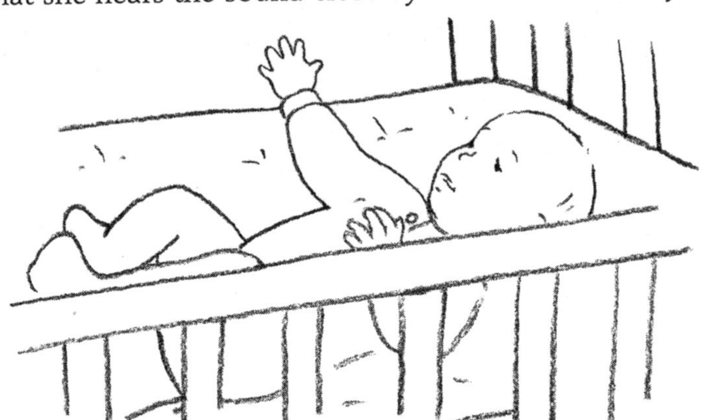

0–3 months

WHAT YOUR BABY WILL LEARN:
About Colors and Shapes

Black and White

- A week after birth, babies can discriminate patterns. Sharply contrasting colors and patterns catch their attention most easily.
- Cut white poster board into 8½" x 11" (21 cm x 27 cm) pieces. Draw designs on the poster board with a wide marker.
- You might also cut out pictures from magazines and tape them to a poster board.
- Arrange the designs and pictures around the crib for the baby to look at. Be sure the baby cannot reach the pictures.

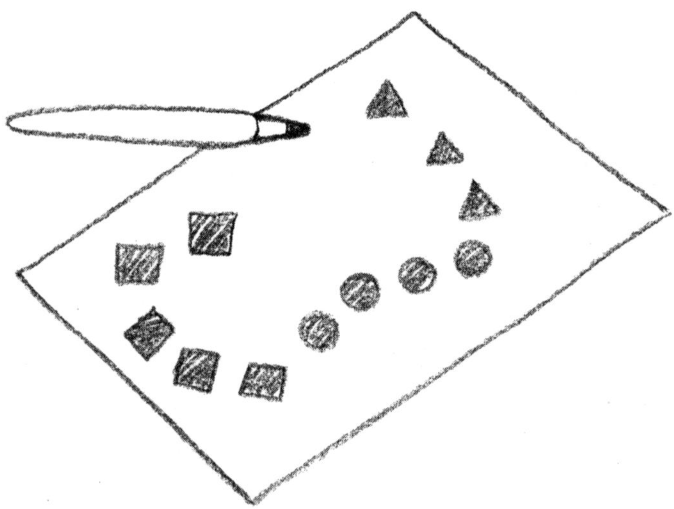

WHAT YOUR BABY WILL LEARN:
Observation Skills

Seeing the World

- Tuck a pillow under your baby's chest. This makes it easier for her to hold up her head and look around.
- Arrange interesting toys in front of the baby.
- Prop an unbreakable mirror in front of her so that she can watch "another baby."
- While a baby lies flat on her stomach, her world is limited. While she is propped up, however, she can use her hands to explore and touch.
- While your baby is propped up, tell her about all the things she sees.

WHAT YOUR BABY WILL LEARN:
About Colors and Shapes

The Umbrella Mobile

- Hang an umbrella upside down at the end of the baby's crib, out of her reach.
- Attach colorful balls, small toys, or bells to the spokes of the umbrella. ***NOTE***: Make certain that the objects are out of baby's reach.
- Stand at that end of the crib and talk to the baby. She will follow your voice with her head.
- Once you have her attention, jiggle the mobile to encourage her to look at all the colors and shapes.
- After you have done this a few times, the baby will look at the mobile by herself.

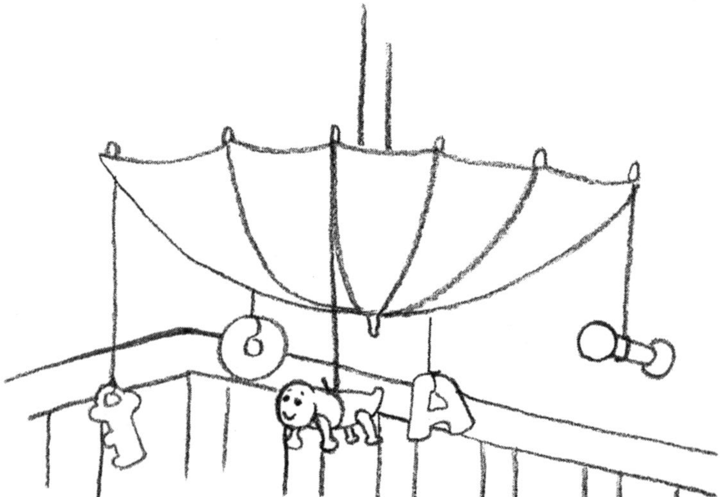

WHAT YOUR BABY WILL LEARN:
Observation Skills

Birdie, Birdie, Tweet, Tweet

- Hold your baby and look into her eyes.
- Slowly wiggle your index finger in front of her eyes to get her attention.
- When you have her attention, wiggle your finger to the left and watch her eyes follow it.
- Wiggle your finger to the right, and see if she continues to follow it with her eyes.
- As you wiggle your finger, say the words, "Birdie, birdie, tweet, tweet."
- At the beginning, your baby may only be able to track your finger for a very short period. Keep doing this daily, and you will see progress.

0–3 months

WHAT YOUR BABY WILL LEARN:
Observation Skills

Mirror Fun

- Put your baby in the crib. The baby's head may be facing forward or to the side.
- Place an unbreakable mirror on the side of the crib.
- Talk to your baby and when you are sure she hears your voice, tap your finger on the mirror to get her attention.
- The mirror will give the baby something stimulating to look at while lying in the crib.

0–3 months

WHAT YOUR BABY WILL LEARN:
Curiosity

What Can I Look At?

- Each time you change your baby's environment, you are giving her an opportunity to look at new things. This will develop her curiosity and her awareness of her environment.
- Hold your baby high so that she can look over your shoulder. Walk around the room and stop at something with a bright color or interesting shape.
- Let the baby look at this object for a few minutes.
- When you put your baby down, be sure there is something interesting for her to look at.

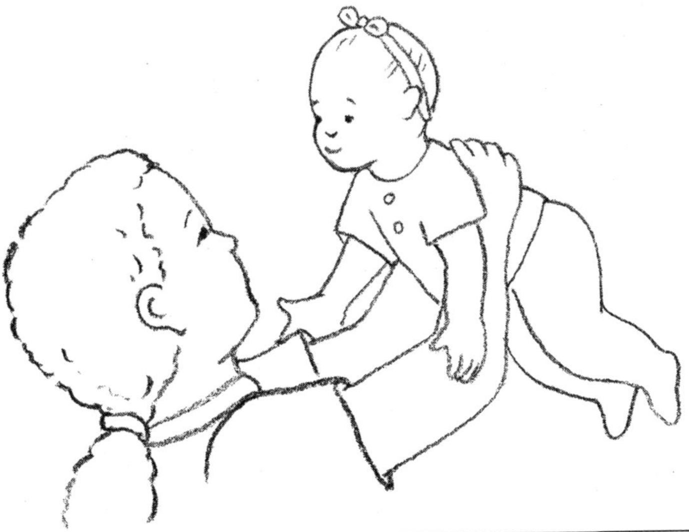

0–3 months

WHAT YOUR BABY WILL LEARN:
To Hold Objects

Hold It Tight

- Hold a small toy in front of your baby where she can see it.
- Touch the inside of her hand with the toy and help her close her fingers around it.
- Take your hand away, leaving her holding the toy.
- When she drops the toy, give it to her again and speak in loving tones.
- Each time, return the toy to the baby's opposite hand.
- As you play this game, your baby's fingers will grow stronger and soon she will be able to open and close her hands voluntarily.
- For tactile experiences, alternate toys that are soft, hard, cool, smooth, and so on.

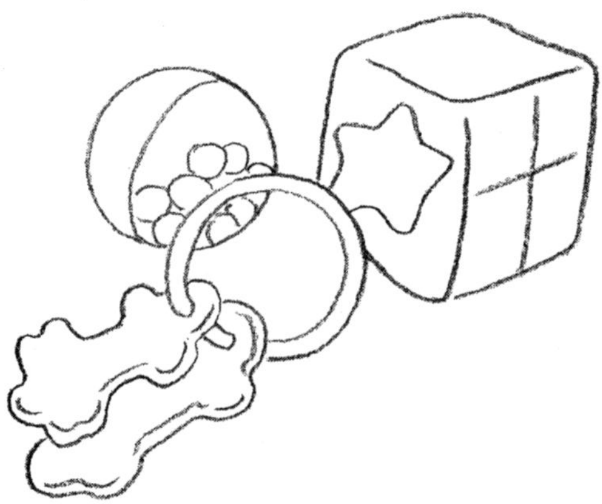

WHAT YOUR BABY WILL LEARN:
Body Awareness

The Hand Discovery

- At about three months of age, babies experience an exciting event—they discover their hands.
- This game will help the process along and provide your baby with endless pleasure.
- Lay the baby on her back and talk softly to her so that you have her complete attention.
- Place her hand gently on her cheek. As you are doing this, say, "Baby's hand is so nice."
- After a few times, hold her hand in front of her eyes before and after you put it on her cheek.
- The baby learns to associate pleasure with seeing her hands.

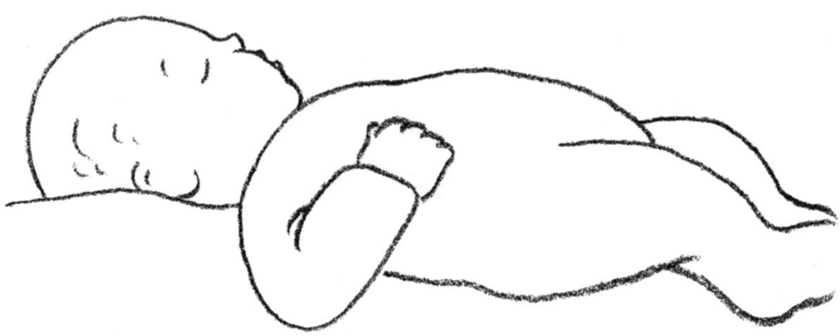

WHAT YOUR BABY WILL LEARN:
About Colors

Oh, How Pretty

- Babies need visual stimulation. Put a brightly colored sock on the baby's foot.
- Move the baby's foot so that she can see the sock.
- When she sees the color, she will get very excited.
- At first, the baby will see colors accidentally, but she will soon learn to concentrate on a color for a longer time.
- Change the sock to her other foot, or put socks on both of her feet.
- Try putting one of the socks on the baby's hand. Watch how she begins to hold her hand in front of her eyes and really concentrate on what she is seeing.

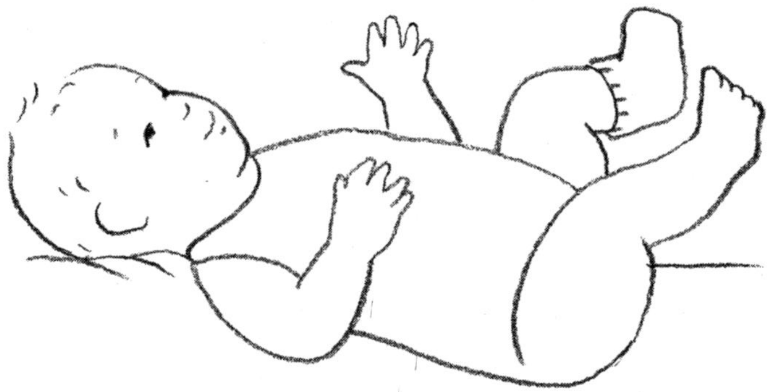

WHAT YOUR BABY WILL LEARN:
About Shapes and Colors

Moving the Picture

- Infants are stimulated by vivid colors in a variety of interesting shapes and patterns.
- Find a colorful picture of an animal and glue it onto a piece of cardboard.
- Punch a hole in the cardboard and thread colorful string through it.
- Tie the picture securely to the bars of the crib where your baby can see it, but make sure it is out of the baby's reach.
- Move the picture to different places in the crib every few days to further stimulate your baby.

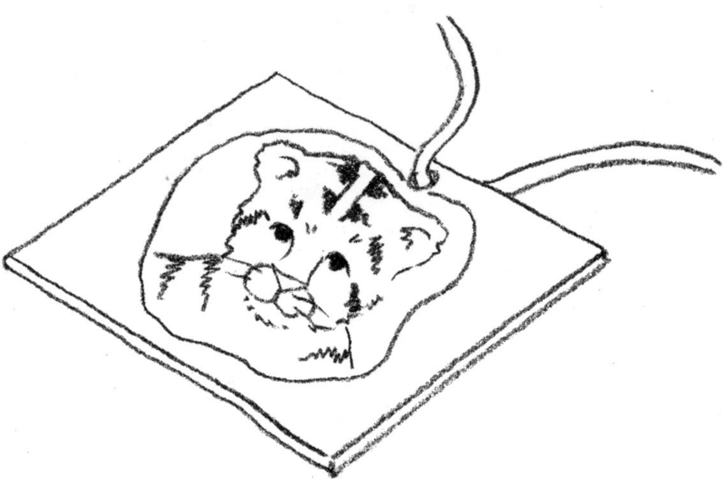

WHAT YOUR BABY WILL LEARN:
Listening Skills

The Tracking Game

- Hold your baby in your lap so that she is facing you. Support her head and help her move it as you play this game.
- Say the baby's name as you move your head from left to right. As you move your head, your baby will follow it with her eyes.
- Keep repeating this game, but change your tone of voice each time you move your head back and forth.
- You can say her name in a soft voice, a whisper, a louder voice, and a happy voice.
- You can also change the expression on your face each time you move back and forth.

0-3 months

WHAT YOUR BABY WILL LEARN:
Visual Exploration

Flashlight Tracking

- This is another way to stimulate your child's vision.
- Hold your baby in your arms in a darkened room.
- Move a flashlight and let your baby follow with her eyes.
- Shine the flashlight on the ceiling, on the floor, and on the wall.
- Shine the flashlight on your hands or your feet.
- Newborn babies need to have their vision stimulated, which builds connections in the brain. Many of a baby's important brain cells need to develop connections before eight months of age.

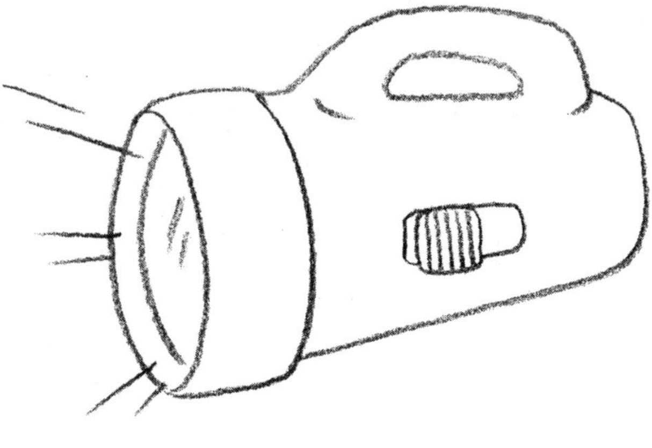

WHAT YOUR BABY WILL LEARN:
To Watch an Object

Puppet Games

- Put a finger puppet on your index finger. Move it around as you say the baby's name.
- Move the puppet up and down, and see whether the baby can follow the movement.
- Slowly move the puppet in a circle.
- Each time that the baby follows the movement, try a new movement.

3–6 months

3–6 months

WHAT YOUR BABY WILL LEARN:
Body Awareness

Sleepy Time

- Recite this rhyme to your baby as you hold him close.

  Sleepy time, little baby
  Sleepy time, little baby
  Sleepy time, little baby
  Here's a kiss for baby.

- When you say, "sleepy time," sway back and forth or move around the room very slowly.
- Kiss the baby in a different place each time.
- Insert the words for different parts of the body into the rhyme.

  Sleepy time, little toesies....
  Sleepy time, little fingers....
  Sleepy time, little tummy....

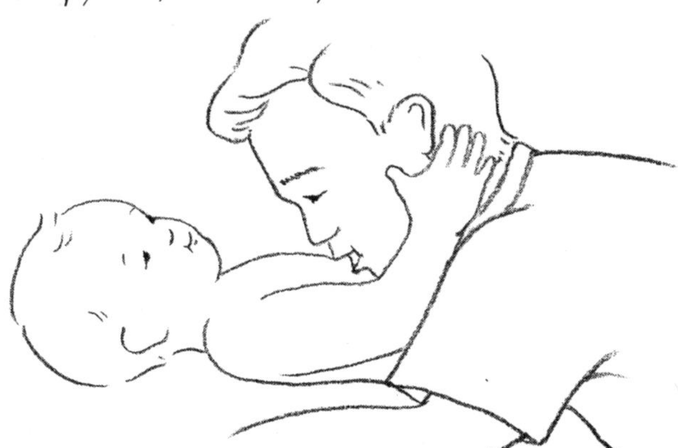

3–6 months

WHAT YOUR BABY WILL LEARN:
Warmth and Trust

Hush-a-Bye

- This is one of the loveliest lullabies I know. It is American in origin, and was first sung in the South.
- If you do not know the melody, say the words in a singsong fashion.
- Rock your baby as you sing. When I sang this to my babies, I changed "sleep" to "sleepy."

Hush-a-bye, don't you cry,
Go to sleep, little baby.
When you wake, you shall take
All the pretty little horses.
Blacks and bays, dapples and grays,
Coach and six little horses.
Hush-a-bye, don't you cry,
Go to sleep, little baby.

- Kiss your baby on the line, "Go to sleep, little baby."

WHAT YOUR BABY WILL LEARN:
Language Skills

Swim Little Fishie

- This game is fun to do in the bathtub or a swimming pool.
- Recite the rhyme while moving your hand under the water like a fish.

Swim, little fishie,
Swim around the pool.
Swim, little fishie,
The water is cool.
Where's the little fishie?
Where did he go?
There he is!
SPLASH, SPLASH!

- Gently splash your baby as you say, "SPLASH, SPLASH!"

3–6 months

WHAT YOUR BABY WILL LEARN:
Language Skills

What's Cooking?

- Whenever you are in the kitchen, sit your baby safely in an infant seat or swing.
- As you prepare food, talk about each thing you do.

  "I'm stirring,"
  "I'm pouring,"
  "I'm washing."

- Let your baby play with measuring spoons, unbreakable bowls, or wooden spoons.
- When your baby is old enough, let him help pour, beat, or stir.
- Always name each ingredient as you use it.

3–6 months

WHAT YOUR BABY WILL LEARN:
About Opposites

All Around the House

- Hold the baby and move about the house as you talk and demonstrate pairs of opposite actions.
- "The light is off...the light is on."

  "The door is open...the door is closed."
  "The towel is on the rack...the towel is on the floor."
  "I'm lifting you up...I'm putting you down."
  "The cup is full...the cup is empty."

- Performing these actions will motivate your baby to do them by himself one day.

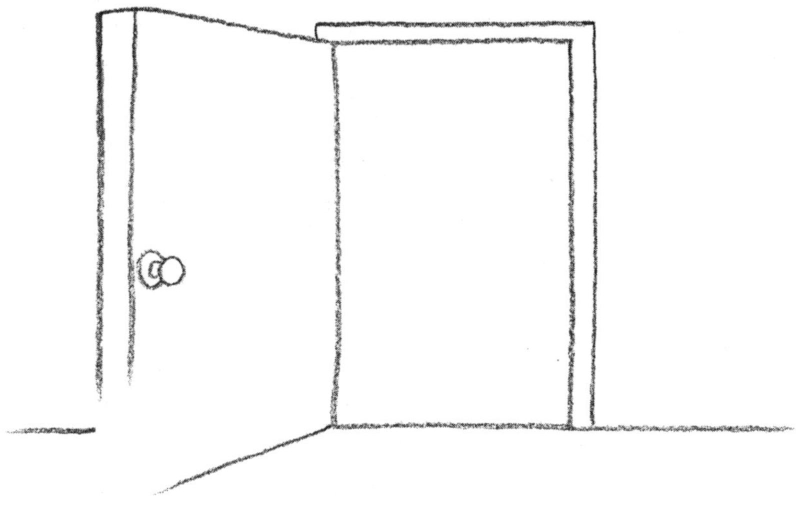

WHAT YOUR BABY WILL LEARN:
Bonding

The Stroking Game

- Babies experience relationships through their senses.
- Touch is particularly important because it stimulates the baby's brain to release growth hormones.
- Stroke your baby's head and say, "I love your head."
- Stroke your baby's back and say, "I love your back."
- Continue stroking your baby and say each body part you touch.
- This kind of loving interaction will help your baby feel safe and secure.

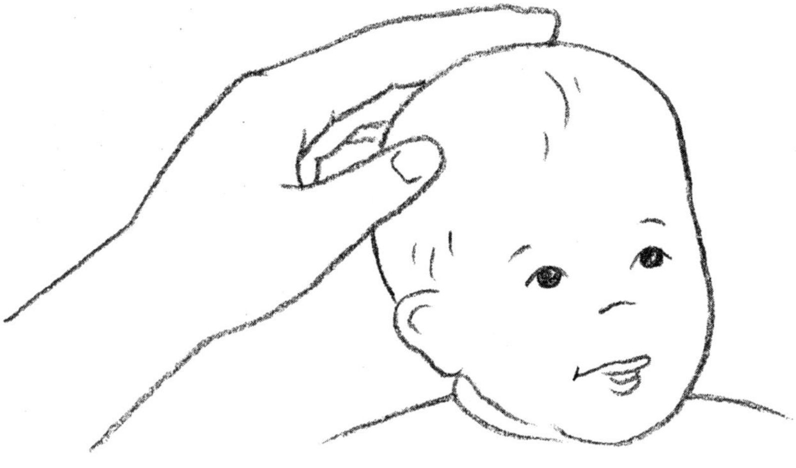

3–6 months

WHAT YOUR BABY WILL LEARN:
Motor Development

Reaching

- Babies at this age are always reaching for things. This is a wonderful opportunity to introduce a physical activity that will help them grow.
- Sit your baby on your lap and give him a favorite toy to hold.
- Play with him by talking to him, jiggling the toy, and making the entire experience very pleasant.
- Now, take the toy and hold it up a little higher than his hand can reach. Encourage him to reach for the toy.
- This will strengthen his muscles.
- Be sure to praise him and give him the toy after he reaches for it.

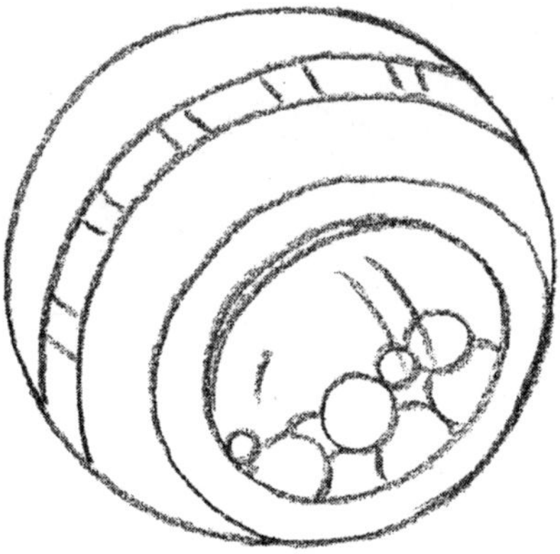

3–6 months

WHAT YOUR BABY WILL LEARN:
Exploration Skills

Exploring

- Lie on the bed and place your baby on your chest.
- Hold the baby firmly and say loving things like, "I love you," "What a sweet baby," and so on.
- Help the baby to explore the parts of your body. When the baby touches your nose, say the word, "Nose." When the baby touches your hair, say the word, "Hair."
- Hold the baby up over your head and say loving things while you look into each other's eyes.

3–6 months

WHAT YOUR BABY WILL LEARN:
Fun

Bumping Noses

- Sit the baby in your lap facing you and say "boo" three times.
- When you say the first and second "boo," move your head toward the baby's. On the third "boo," bump noses with the baby. If you say the last "boo" a little louder, it makes the game even more fun.
- Repeat this over and over. Change the tone of your voice each time. Sometimes use a high voice, and sometimes use a low voice.
- Try whispering the first and second "boo," then say the third "boo" in a normal voice. Be careful not to shout as this might scare the baby.

3–6 months

WHAT YOUR BABY WILL LEARN:
Body Awareness

Baby's Fingers

- This game develops body awareness and vocabulary. It also provides a wonderful opportunity to bond with your baby.
- While you dress your baby, you have the perfect opportunity to talk about different parts of the body.
- Gently touch each of the baby's fingers. As you do so, say in a singsong voice, "This is (child's name)'s finger."
- Place the baby's hand on your finger. In the same voice, say, "This is (say your name here)'s finger."

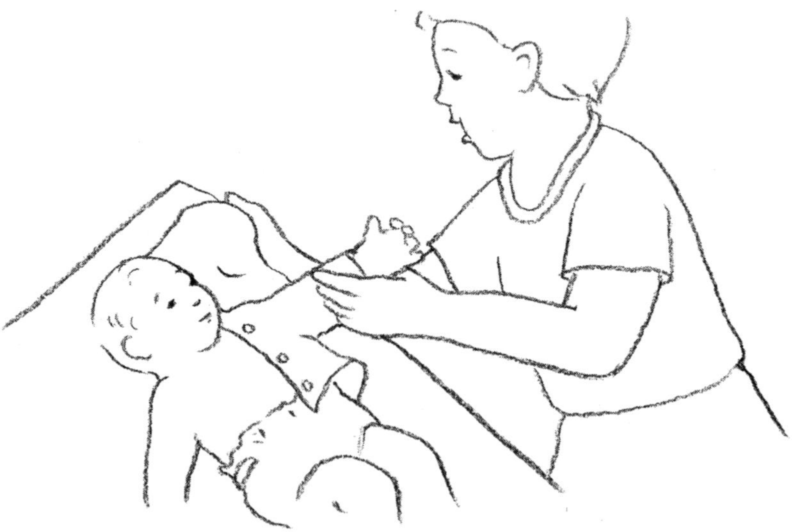

WHAT YOUR BABY WILL LEARN:
About Colors

Hello, Hands

- Babies at this age like to explore their hands and feet, so they really enjoy this game.
- Take a pair of your baby's socks and cut five holes into each sock for fingers.
- Decorate the socks with bright colors (use non-toxic materials or markers) and interesting shapes or faces.
- Fit the socks onto the baby's hands for him to look at, talk to, and enjoy.
- Remember to choose decorations cautiously because the baby will most likely put his hands in his mouth.

WHAT YOUR BABY WILL LEARN:
Coordination

Fascinating Toes

- Infants love to look at their fingers and toes. This delightful game gives them a new perspective.
- Take your baby's sock (plain white is preferred) and decorate it with colors, yarn, or even attach a bell. Use nontoxic materials and securely fasten them.
- Put the sock on the baby's foot and watch the excitement that follows.
- Do not leave the baby unattended because he might put the sock in his mouth.

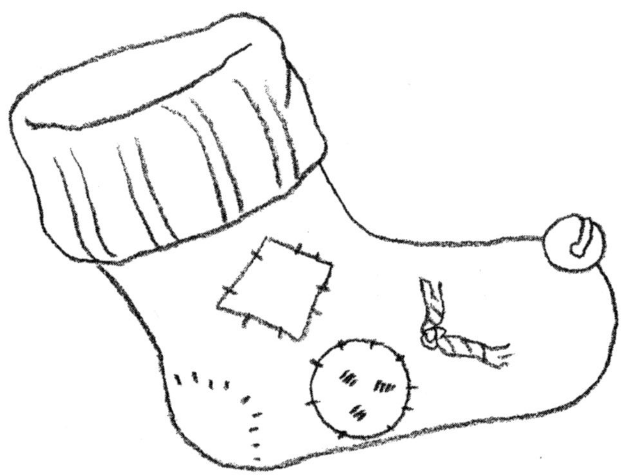

WHAT YOUR BABY WILL LEARN:
Fun

This Little Toe

- Gently rub each of baby's toes as you recite this rhyme.

  This little toe goes a rub-a-dub-dub.
  This little toe goes a scrub-a-scrub-scrub.
  Rub-a-dub-dub,
  Scrub-a-scrub-scrub,
  This little toe goes
  SPLASH!

- Change your voice when you say "SPLASH!"
- Each time you play this game, change the way you say "SPLASH!" Speak in a high voice, a low voice, a soft voice, or a whisper.

3–6 months

WHAT YOUR BABY WILL LEARN:
About Parts of the Body

Fingers and Toes

- Say the following rhyme. Each time you say the word "fingers," wiggle your baby's fingers.
- Each time you say the word "toes," wiggle your baby's toes.

Fingers and toes, fingers and toes
Here are your fingers
And here are your toes.
Wiggle your fingers
Wiggle your toes
Here are your fingers
And here are your toes.
Wave with your fingers
Wave with your toes
Here are your fingers
And here are your toes.

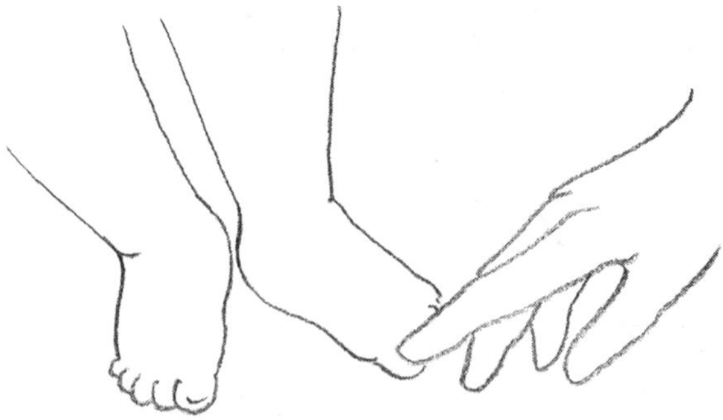

3–6 months

WHAT YOUR BABY WILL LEARN:
Body Awareness

Five Little Fingers

- Hold your baby's fingers in your hand. Move one finger back and forth and say, "Wiggle little finger."
- Do this with each finger.
- Repeat the same steps, wiggling the baby's toes.
- Recite this rhyme to the baby as you wiggle his fingers or toes.

What can I do with five little fingers?
What can I do with five little fingers?
What can I do with five little fingers?
What can I do today?
I can wiggle my five little fingers.
I can wiggle my five little fingers.
I can wiggle my five little fingers.
I can wiggle them today.

- Also try shaking, waving, or clapping your baby's five little fingers.

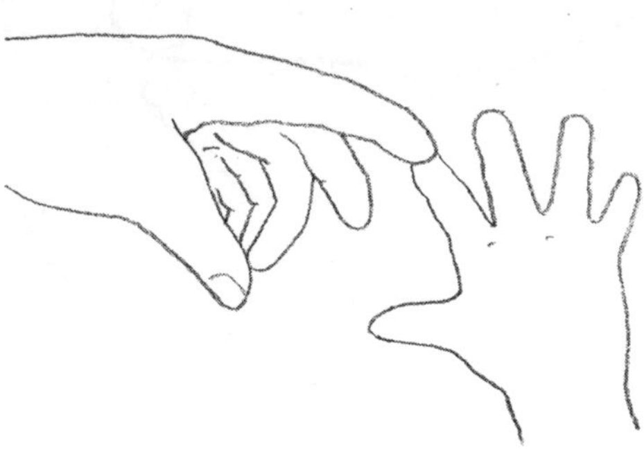

3–6 months

WHAT YOUR BABY WILL LEARN:
Body Awareness

Touch Your Fingers

- Cradle your baby's hand in yours and gently stroke each finger, saying "Finger."
- Gently stroke each toe, saying "Toe."
- Place your baby's fingers on his toes.
- Tap his fingers on his toes and say, "Fingers on toes, fingers on toes."
- Count the baby's fingers or toes.

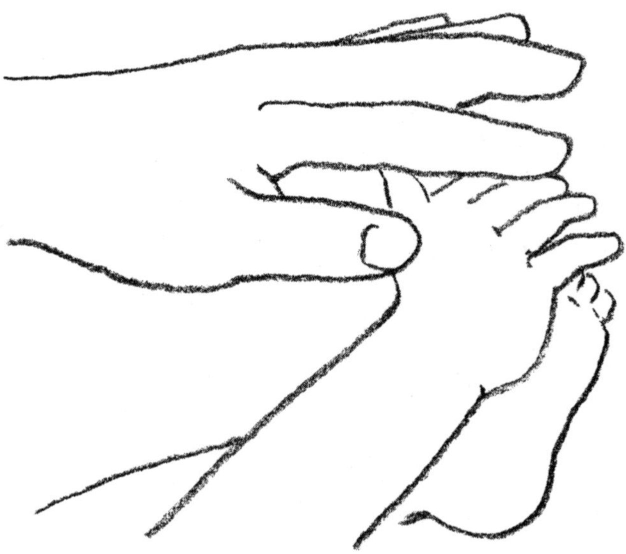

3–6 months

WHAT YOUR BABY WILL LEARN:
Bonding

This Little Piggy

- Babies love to play with their fingers and toes. Touch each finger or toe as you recite this poem.

  This little piggy went to market,
  This little piggy stayed home,
  This little piggy had roast beef,
  This little piggy had none,
  And this little piggy went, "Wee, wee, wee,"
  All the way home.

- Before you say, "Wee, wee, wee," slow down to build suspense. Then say the last line faster than the rest.
- On the "wee, wee, wee," you can do many things. Tickle the baby, dance around while holding the baby, or gently shake the baby's hand or foot.
- Another variation is to say, "Wee, wee, wee" in different voices—high, low, happy, sad, and so on.

3–6 months

WHAT YOUR BABY WILL LEARN:
Dexterity

Where Is Thumbkin?

- Babies adore this popular singing game.

Where is Thumbkin?
Where is Thumbkin?
Here I am, here I am.
How are you today, sir?
Very well, I thank you.
Run away, run away.
Where is pointer...
Where is tall one...
Where is ringman...
Where is pinky...
Where's the whole family...

- Start singing and keep both hands behind your back. Bring out one thumb when you reach "Here I am." Bring out the other thumb at the second "Here I am."
- Wiggle one thumb on the line, "How are you today, sir" and wiggle the other thumb on the line, "Very well, I thank you."
- On the words "Run away," put your thumbs behind your back, one at a time.
- Start the second verse with both hands behind your back. Repeat the same actions for each of the fingers: index, middle, ring, and pinky. "The whole family" means all five fingers together.

3–6 months

WHAT YOUR BABY WILL LEARN:
Coordination

Kick Those Legs

- Put your baby on his back.
- Hold his legs at the ankles and bend them at the knee.
- Straighten his legs, one at a time, and repeat this kicking movement several times.
- Next, bring the two legs together and kick them together.
- Singing a song while you do this exercise makes it more fun for the baby.

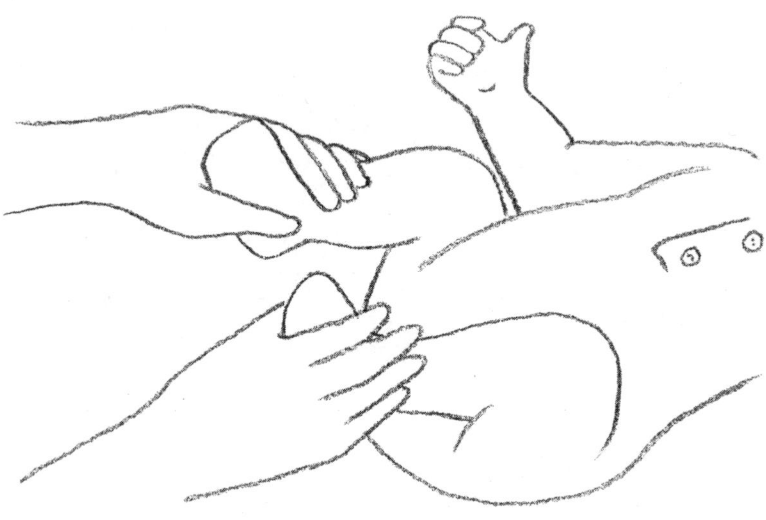

WHAT YOUR BABY WILL LEARN:
Rolling

The Rolling Surprise

- Lay your baby next to you on a soft surface.
- Pick out two colorful toys that he will enjoy looking at.
- Put one of the toys on each side of the baby.
- Say to your baby, "It's time to roll."
- Gently roll him over to one side so that he can look at the toy, reach for it, and respond to it.
- Then roll him over to the other side so that he will see a different toy.
- This game will encourage him to roll side to side.

3–6 months

WHAT YOUR BABY WILL LEARN:
Trust

Up and Down the Elevator

- Lift your baby up over your head and bring him down slowly to your face.
- When your faces touch, say, "I love you."
- Lift your baby into the air as you say, "Time to go up the elevator. Bye-bye."
- Bring your baby down as you say, "Time to come down the elevator," and kiss him on the cheek.

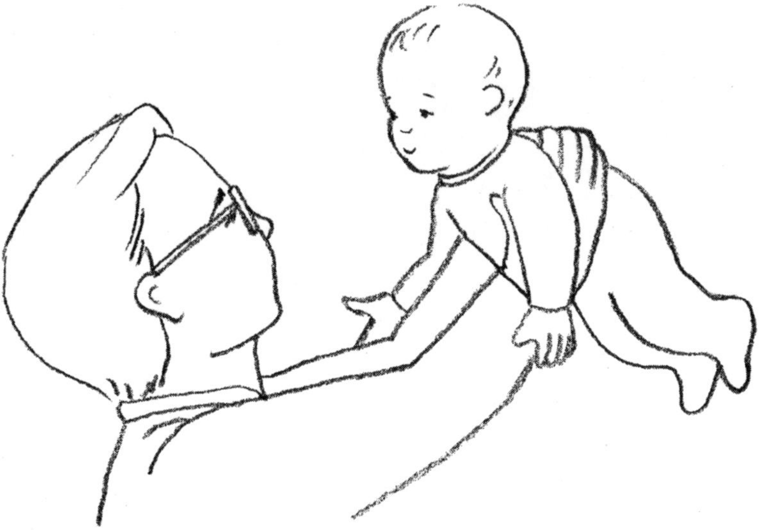

3–6 months

WHAT YOUR BABY WILL LEARN:
Balance

Bouncy, Bouncy

- Sit on a comfortable chair with your legs crossed.
- Sit the baby on your legs and grasp him under his arms.
- Move your legs up and down and recite this rhyme.

Bouncy, bouncy baby.
Bouncy, bouncy baby.
Up and down, up and down,
Bouncy, bouncy baby.
Hippety hop, bippety bop,
Bouncy, bouncy BOOM.

- When you say, "BOOM," lift the baby up and give him a big hug.

3–6 months

WHAT YOUR BABY WILL LEARN:
Bonding

Fly, Baby, Fly

- Sit on the floor with your baby facing you. Support the baby's body by placing your hands firmly under his arms and around his chest.
- Ask your baby, "Are you ready to fly in the sky?" Then say, "Here we go. One, two, threeeee!"
- On the count of three, slowly begin lifting the baby as you roll backward onto your back.
- You are now lying down and holding the baby "high in the sky." Say, "Fly, baby, fly!" "Whee," or whatever else you can think of.
- This is a very good game to strengthen your back muscles.

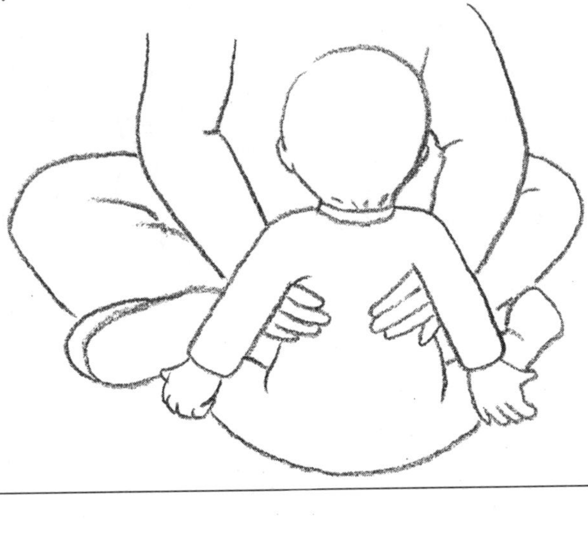

3–6 months

WHAT YOUR BABY WILL LEARN:
A Sense of Humor

Diaper Fun

- Games like this one develop a child's sense of humor.
- Make diaper-changing fun. Hold the diaper in front of your face, then take it away and say, "Peek-a-boo."
- Hold the diaper in front of your face, bend your head down next to the baby's head and say, "Peek-a-boo" in a soft voice.
- Wave the diaper back and forth in front of your face and say, "Peek-a-boo."

3–6 months

WHAT YOUR BABY WILL LEARN:
Anticipation

The Spider Game

- This game is a lot of fun.
- Lie on the floor with your baby, on your tummies, facing each other.
- Make your fingers crawl like a spider. Make them disappear and reappear. Wiggle your fingers.
- Crawl your fingers over your baby's hands, then make them disappear. Always say, "Here comes the spider!"
- Crawl your fingers on your baby's nose, then make them disappear. Always say, "Here comes the spider!"

3–6 months

WHAT YOUR BABY WILL LEARN:
Anticipation

Here Comes a Bug

- Sit your baby in a chair or on the floor facing you.
- Wiggle your fingers across the chair or floor, coming closer and closer to the baby.
- As you are wiggling say, "Here comes the bug, buggy, buggy, bug."
- When you get close to the baby, "jump" your fingers onto his toe or finger.
- Say the word "jump" as your hand leaps toward him.

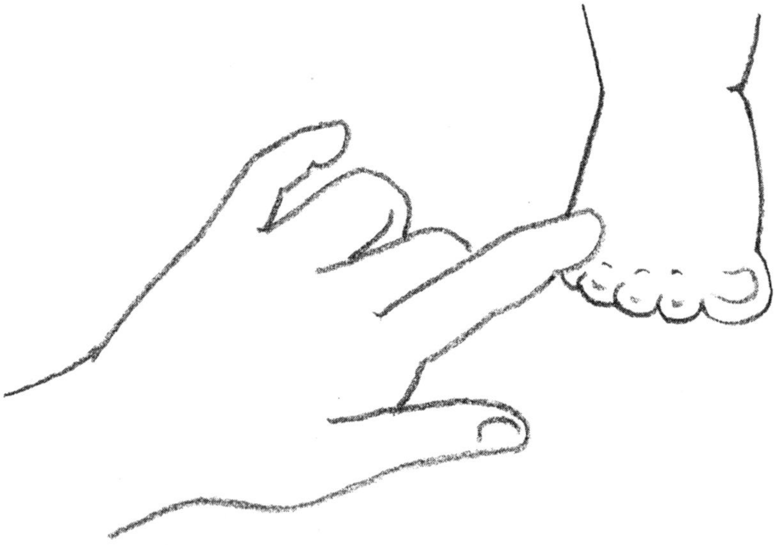

WHAT YOUR BABY WILL LEARN:
Body Awareness

Cockle Doodle Doo

- Children love this game because of the words "cockle doodle doo."

Put your hand on your head,
Cockle doodle doo.
Put your hand on your ear,
Cockle doodle doo.
Put your hand on your nose,
Cockle doodle doo.
Put your hand on your cheek,
Cockle doodle doo.

- Hold your baby as you say the words and put his hand on the parts of the body that you mention.
- Name familiar things, then place your baby's hand on them.

Put your hand on your bottle....
Put your hand on the table....
Put your hand on the spoon....

3–6 months

WHAT YOUR BABY WILL LEARN:
To Eat from a Spoon

Here's the Spoon!

- When your baby first sees a spoon, he may not know what it is for.
- Show him the spoon without any food.
- Hold the spoon in front of him, raise it to your mouth, and pretend to eat, saying, "Yum, yum, yum."
- Now place some food on the spoon and hold it to your baby's mouth. Feed him the food.
- Soon he will understand what the spoon is for, and become very excited each time he sees it.

3–6 months

WHAT YOUR BABY WILL LEARN:
Hand-Eye Coordination

Hand Fun

- When your baby is able to sit comfortably in a high chair, you can start giving him small bits of food to pick up.
- Dry cereal and diced cooked vegetables will challenge your baby and develop his dexterity.
- Put some dry cereal on the baby's high chair and show him how to pick one up and put it down again. (Putting it down is the hard part.)
- Show your baby how to pick up a piece of food and place it in the other hand.
- Hold out your hand, palm up, and see if your baby can pick up a piece of food and place it into your hand.

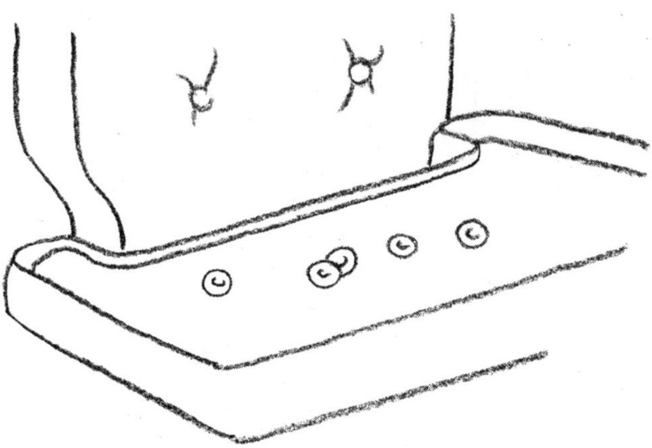

3–6 months

WHAT YOUR BABY WILL LEARN:
Exploration Skills

Jelly in the Bowl

- Playing with Jell-O® is a wonderful way to introduce babies to texture.
- Mix Jell-O® and allow it to set. Cut it into blocks and put them on your baby's tray. He will love watching the Jell-O® squirm and move around.
- This is an old and popular rhyme. Recite it as you play with the Jell-O®.

  Jelly in the bowl,
  Jelly in the bowl,
  Wibble wobble, wibble wobble,
  Jelly in the bowl.

- Change the word "jelly" to "Jell-O®."

WHAT YOUR BABY WILL LEARN:
About Textures

Baby's Bottle

- If your baby drinks from a bottle, this activity can help him experience different textures.
- Put a bottle cover on the bottle and let him feel it as he sucks.
- Use a sock instead of a commercial bottle cover.
- Experiment with different fabrics and see which ones your baby enjoys.

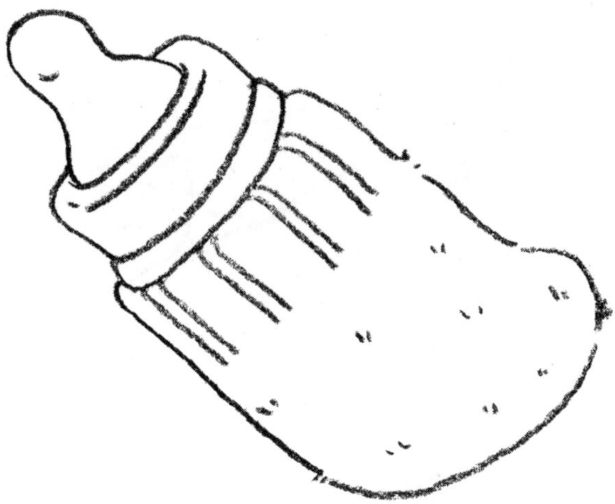

3–6 months

WHAT YOUR BABY WILL LEARN:
Hand-Eye Coordination

Reach Out and Touch

- Tie a scarf around your neck so that the ends dangle in front of you.
- Lean over your baby so that he can see your face and reach the scarf.
- Slowly shake the scarf to attract his attention. Touch his hands with the scarf.
- As the baby reaches for the scarf, smile and talk to him to let him know you are happy with what he is doing.

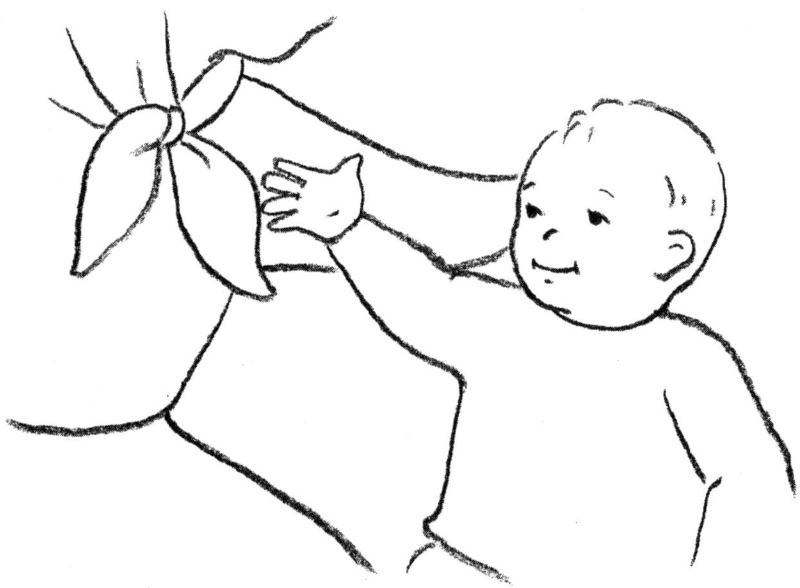

3–6 months

WHAT YOUR BABY WILL LEARN:
About Textures

How Does It Feel?

- Punch two finger holes into a narrow box.
- Line the box with materials of different textures—fur, burlap, velvet, or sandpaper. Tape the box closed.
- Show the baby how to poke a finger through a hole. Poke your finger into the other hole.
- Talk to the baby about how the materials feel. Are they soft, rough, or bumpy?
- This is a good game to play in the car.

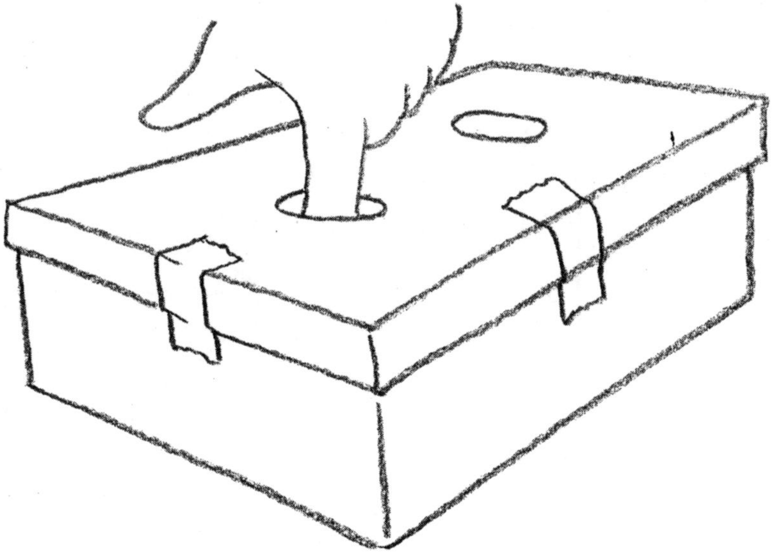

WHAT YOUR BABY WILL LEARN:
Rhythm

Tapping Away

- Babies love to bang on things. This kind of activity develops the baby's hearing and listening skills.
- Mealtime provides a perfect opportunity to encourage these skills.
- Put your baby in a high chair and give him a wooden spoon. Watch how he immediately starts tapping everything around him.
- Grab a wooden spoon and join in the fun.
- As you tap along with your baby, sing the words "Tap, tap, tapping."
- This game is great fun and develops language skills as well.

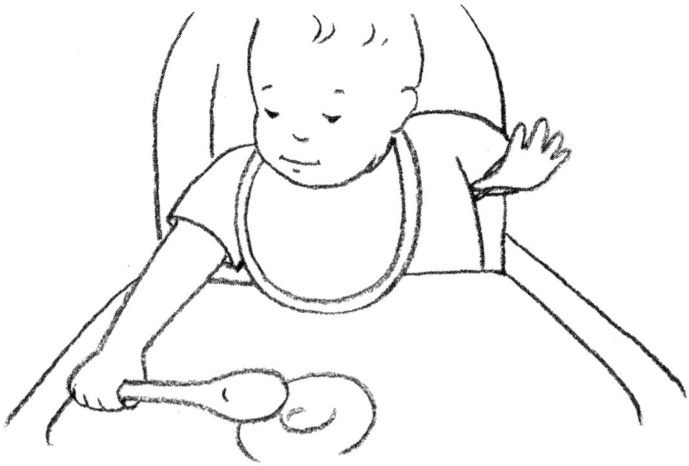

3–6 months

WHAT YOUR BABY WILL LEARN:
Pre-Reading Skills

Rhythm Talk

- The rhythm of syllables helps infants learn where one word ends and another word begins.
- Recite lots of nursery rhymes and poems to your baby.
- Pick a favorite poem and repeat it in different ways.
- Hold your baby's hands as you say the rhyme.
- Sway back and forth as you say the rhyme.
- Tap your baby's fingers on your face as you say the rhyme.
- The more words babies hear, the sooner they will speak.

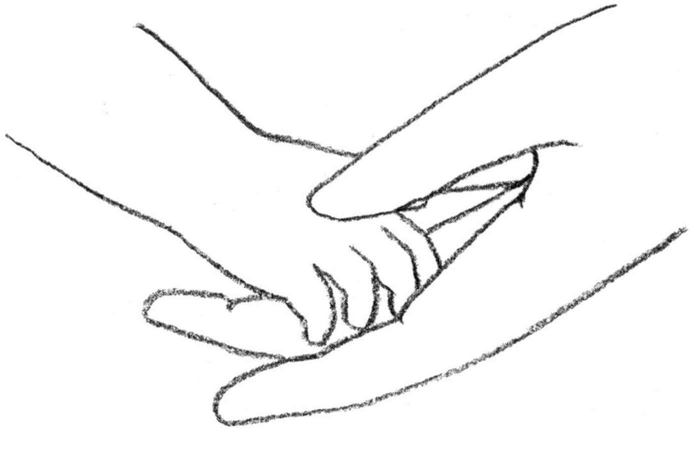

3–6 months

WHAT YOUR BABY WILL LEARN:
About Sounds

Shake, Shake, Shake

- Fill several small plastic containers with different objects like bells, dry beans, rice, or marbles. Film canisters and plastic eggs make good containers. ***NOTE***: Fasten the lids **securely** so that the baby cannot remove the contents.
- Give a container to the baby and while holding the baby's hand, shake the container and say, "Shake, shake."
- Then give the baby another container and do the same thing.
- This is a beginning game that encourages babies to discriminate among sounds which, in turn, promotes language development.

3–6 months

WHAT YOUR BABY WILL LEARN:
About Sounds

Where's the Sound?

- Give the baby a rattle and help him shake it. See whether he can shake it by himself.
- Place the rattle in his other hand. Help him shake it, then see if he can shake it by himself.
- Watch to see whether his eyes focus on the source of the sound.
- Shake the rattle while saying, "Shake, shake, rattle, shake."
- Give the baby the rattle and repeat those words as he shakes the rattle.
- Continue this game to help your baby realize that it is his hand doing the shaking.

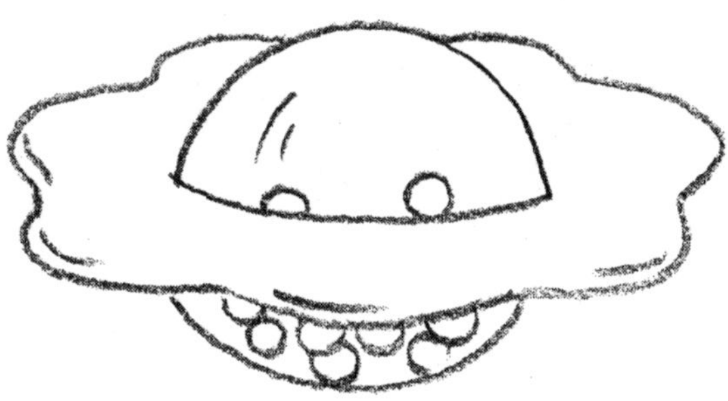

3–6 months

WHAT YOUR BABY WILL LEARN:
Imitation

Silly Sounds

- Sit your baby in your lap facing you.
- Make funny sounds and shapes with your mouth.

  Shape your lips like a fish and smack them.
  Stick out your tongue and wiggle it.
  Shape your mouth into a circle and make a funny sound.

- These sights and sounds will make your baby laugh. He will also try to imitate you.

3–6 months

WHAT YOUR BABY WILL LEARN:
Language Skills

Sing, Sing, Sing

- Sing to your baby about everything. Make up your own tunes and sing about objects in the room, things you see on car trips, and cleaning. Wherever you are and whatever you do can become a song.
- Here are some samples that you could sing to the tune of "Row, Row, Row Your Boat."

Let's go to the store
On this rainy day.
We will buy some food to eat,
And then go home again.
Let's clean up the room,
Lots of things to do.
Make it look so clean and bright,
Now it looks just right.
Let's go to the kitchen,
Are you hungry now?
Apples, peas and bread and jelly
And some milk to drink.

- The words do not have to rhyme. Just sing about everyday things with a positive attitude.

3–6 months

WHAT YOUR BABY WILL LEARN:
About Sounds

Twinkle, Twinkle

- One of the first things that infants learn is to recognize sounds. Helping your baby differentiate the sounds he hears will further his development.
- Hold your baby in your arms and sing a song such as "Twinkle, Twinkle, Little Star."
- Sing the song in different voices, sometimes high and sometimes low.
- Change the baby's position as you sing to him, such as over one shoulder, then the other shoulder, and so on.

WHAT YOUR BABY WILL LEARN:
Language Skills

Talk to Me, Baby

- When babies begin to talk, it is called babbling. Babies make all kinds of sounds as they experiment with moving their tongues around in their mouths.
- First sounds like "da, da, da" are exciting for parents. When your baby says "Da, da, da," answer him with the same sounds.
- If you answer the baby, he will probably repeat the sound.
- Repeat the sounds the baby makes. This will encourage him to babble more and more, because he enjoys communicating with you.
- While you are playing this game, make a new sound and see if the baby will imitate you. Try "mo, mo, mo" or "dee, dee, dee."

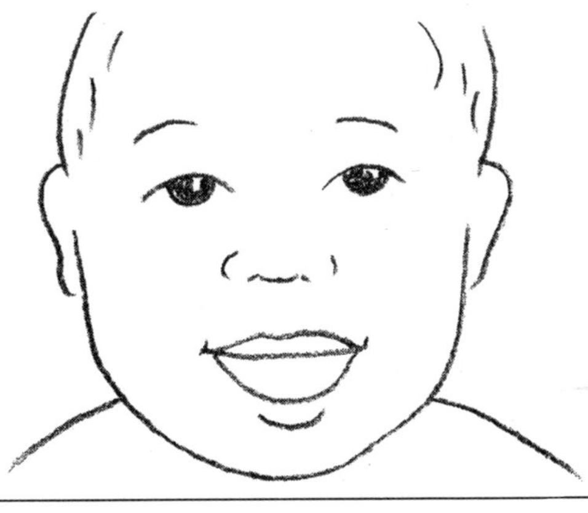

WHAT YOUR BABY WILL LEARN:
Language Development

Talking to Your Baby

- Sit down with your baby and look into his eyes.
- Start a conversation about anything. You can talk about what you are having for dinner, about members of the family, or anything else relating to your baby.
- As your baby responds with coos and other sounds, copy these sounds and include them in your conversation.
- Even though your baby cannot understand all of your words, this will help him learn many new words that will form the foundation for his language development.
- As he grows older, you will be amazed at the vocabulary he has acquired.

3–6 months

WHAT YOUR BABY WILL LEARN

Language Skills

The Name Game

- Babies are curious about their environment. They like to peek at, examine, and touch everything around them.
- It is important to name the objects that you give to your baby, such as "Here is your rattle" or "Let's put on your hat."
- As you name objects, your baby will begin to learn language.
- Take three familiar objects and put them in front of your baby. Ask him, "Where is your hat?"
- Pick up the hat and give it to him, saying, "Here is your hat."

3–6 months

WHAT YOUR BABY WILL LEARN:
Body Awareness

The Body Game

- Hold your baby in your lap. Touch different features of his face and name each one.
- Touch two features. Each time say, "This is (child's name)'s nose," "This is (child's name)'s cheek." Repeat several times.
- Take your baby's hand and place it on your nose and cheek alternately. As you guide his hand, say, "This is Daddy's nose," and "This is Daddy's cheek."
- If you touch and name only two features at a time, it will be much easier for the baby to begin to understand the words.
- Now ask the baby, "Where's your nose?" Place his hand on his nose and say, "Here it is!" Repeat this with all of your features that you named.

WHAT YOUR BABY WILL LEARN:
Language Skills

Talk, Talk, Talk

- As babies reach the age of five to six months, before they understand words, they respond to many visual cues.
- Talk to your baby, and always tell him what you are going to do before you do it.
- Say to him, "I am going to pick you up." Then stretch out your arms to offer a visual cue.
- Tell the baby things in advance: "I'm going to put you down." "I'm going to change your diaper." "I'm going to give you a kiss."
- After you have done this for awhile, instead of saying an entire sentence, just say one word: "up," "down," and so forth.

- Your baby will soon respond to your cues. If you hold out your arms and say the word "up" each time you are going to pick up the baby, he will soon stretch out his arms when he sees your arms stretched out.

3–6 months

WHAT YOUR BABY WILL LEARN:
To Concentrate

Look, Look, Look

- Some research suggests that the more infants are encouraged to look at new objects, the higher they will score on intelligence tests at age four.
- Moving your infant to different rooms and to different levels (floor, chair, bed) can make a big difference in what he sees.
- Pick three objects. Hold one object in your hand and tell the baby the name of the object. Do the same with the other two objects.
- Put each object in your baby's hand, one by one, and say each name again.
- The next time you offer the baby the same objects, repeat the game.
- A variation of this game is to put the object behind your back and say to the baby, "Where is the ____________?" Then move the object from behind your back and say, "Here it is."

3–6 months

WHAT YOUR BABY WILL LEARN:
Memory

Remembering

- Place two blocks in front of your baby. Choose blocks that are totally different in appearance.
- Describe the block to your baby as you pick it up. Say, "This is the red block."
- Take the red block and put it behind your back.
- Make sure that your baby sees where you put the block.
- Ask your baby, "Where is the red block?"
- He will give you a sign that he knows where it is. Pointing and making sounds are two ways that your infant can communicate with you.

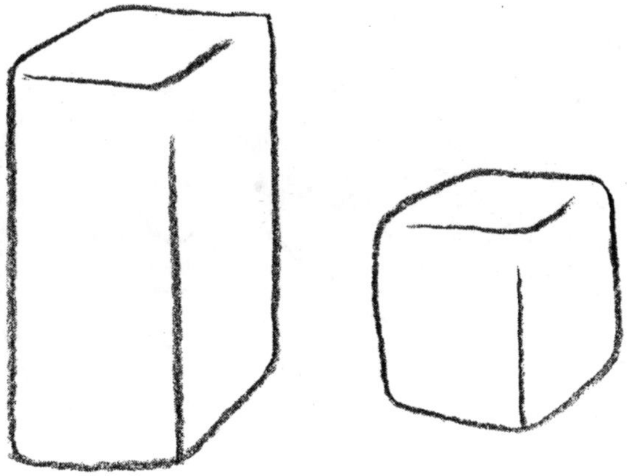

WHAT YOUR BABY WILL LEARN:
Language Skills

Roly-Poly Books

- Turn a round container, like an oatmeal box, into a book for your baby.
- Cut out attractive pictures from magazines and paste them on the box. Select pictures of things that are familiar to your baby, such as animals, people, cups, balls, or toys.
- Cover the pictures with clear contact paper.
- Play with your baby. Roll the box, and point to the different pictures. Talk about them.
- Ask your baby to find a picture, "Where's the doggie?"

6–9 months

WHAT YOUR BABY WILL LEARN:
Trust

Relieving Stress

- Holding and cuddling a baby is a great stress reliever for adults.
- Your baby feels safe and secure in your arms, and you are silently communicating trust.
- As your baby grows more independent, she will sometimes want to hold her own bottle.
- Continue to hold her while she holds her bottle.
- Talk softly and gently to your baby as you hold her. You can also rock her and sing quietly.

WHAT YOUR BABY WILL LEARN:
Security

A New Peek-a-boo

- Put your baby in her infant seat.
- Move out of the room while she is watching you. Then come right back into the room and say, "Peek-a-boo (your child's name)" in a lively voice.
- Your baby will be delighted and will anticipate your return.
- Put a favorite toy in her lap.
- Play the game again, saying "Peek-a-boo" to the toy.
- Use the name of the toy in your sentence.
- This game teaches trust.

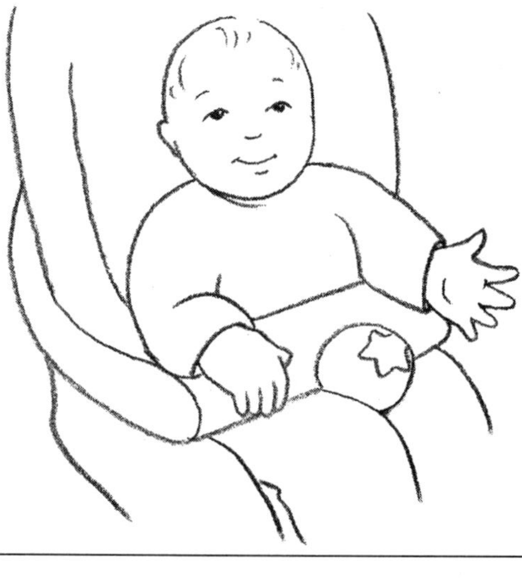

WHAT YOUR BABY WILL LEARN:
A Sense of Humor

The Napkin Game

- Babies adore this game and will play it for long periods.
- Sit the baby on your lap facing you.
- Place a dinner napkin made of soft material on your head, partially covering your face.
- Take the napkin off and say, "Peek-a-boo."
- Do this several times before trying it on the baby. Then put the napkin on the baby's head, pull it off, and say, "Peek-a-boo."
- Put the napkin on the baby's head and see if she will pull it off herself. Keep pulling it off until she learns to do it herself.

6–9 months

WHAT YOUR BABY WILL LEARN:
Exploration Skills

Which Hand Is It?

- Close your hand around a small, interesting object.
- Open your hand to show the baby the toy. Close your hand.
- Ask the baby, "Where's the (name of object)?" Open your hand again to show the object to the baby.
- Using your other hand, repeat the game.
- Soon your baby will grab your hand to try to reach the object.
- This game helps babies understand that objects placed inside containers do not disappear.

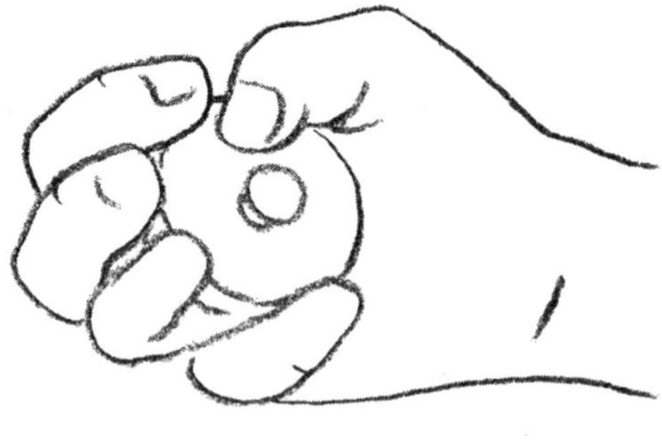

6–9 months

WHAT YOUR BABY WILL LEARN:
Exercise

Backstroke Baby

- This bath time game usually delights babies.
- Fill the baby's bath with a very small amount of water.
- Lay the baby on her back in the bath and let her kick.
- Keep your hand on the baby's head so she won't get water in her ears.
- Praise the baby as she kicks her legs.

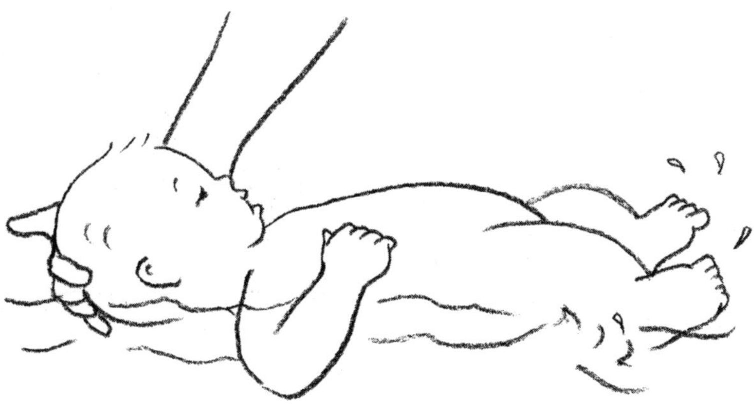

WHAT YOUR BABY WILL LEARN:
Language Skills

Who Do You See?

- Changing a baby's diaper is a wonderful opportunity to share a special time with her and help her development.
- Put pictures on walls near the changing table so that she can look at them while you change her diaper.
- Start with pictures of family members. When she looks at them, ask her, "Who do you see?"
- Always name the person in the picture.
- Hang pictures of animals, and ask the child the name of the animal and what sound it makes.

WHAT YOUR BABY WILL LEARN:
Fun

Zip, Zip, Zip

- Diapering a baby gets harder as she gets older. Reciting a special poem will keep the baby's attention.

  Zip, zip, zip, off it goes!
  I see baby without clothes.
  Zip, zip, what do I see?
  Diaper on, one, two, three!

- Trying to say "zip" is great fun for the baby.

6–9 months

WHAT YOUR BABY WILL LEARN:
Fun

Rattle, Rattle, Rattle, Rattle, Bing!

- Infants like to study their hands and feet.
- They like to put their hands and feet into their mouths, shake and wiggle them, and touch things with them.
- Take a favorite soft rattle and put it in your baby's hand. Shake her hand with the rattle and say, "Rattle, rattle, rattle, rattle, bing!"
- On the word "bing," touch your finger gently to your baby's nose.
- Now put the rattle on your baby's toes and play the same game.

6–9 months

WHAT YOUR BABY WILL LEARN:
The Names of Parts of the Body

Where's Your Toe?

- This is a wonderful game to teach your baby about body parts and establish a loving bond between the two of you.
- Sit your baby in your lap and say the following:

> *Where's your toe?*
> *Here it is.* (Touch her toe and kiss it.)
> *I love your toe*
> *Very much.*
> *Where's your nose?*
> *Here it is.* (Touch her nose and kiss it.)
> *I love your nose*
> *Very much.*

- Continue the game, naming different body parts.

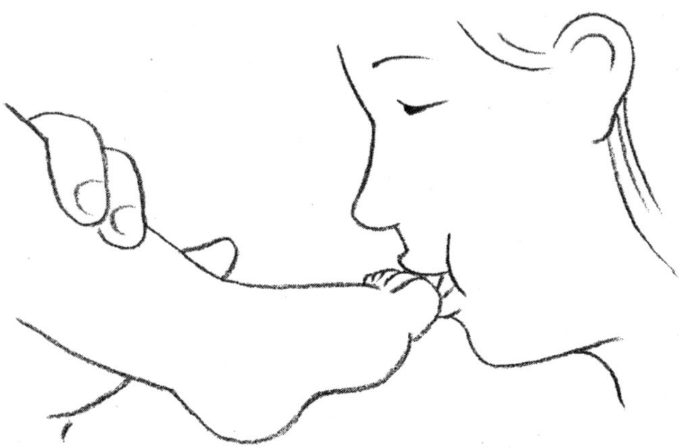

6–9 months

WHAT YOUR BABY WILL LEARN:
Bonding

Pinkety Pinkety

- Recite this rhyme while playing with the baby's thumbs.

Pinkety, pinkety, thumb to thumb,
Wish a wish, and it's sure to come. (Put your thumbs on the baby's thumbs.)
If yours come true, mine will come true, (Wrap your thumbs around the baby's thumbs.)
Pinkety, pinkety, thumb to thumb. (Kiss the baby's thumbs.)

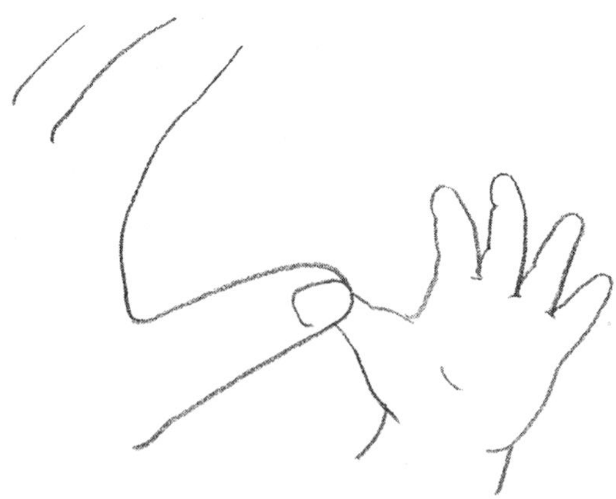

6–9 months

WHAT YOUR BABY WILL LEARN:
About Animal Sounds

Creeping

- Creep your fingers up the baby's arm as you recite this rhyme.

  Creeping, creeping, creeping
  Comes the little cat.
  Meow, meow, meow, meow,
  Meow, meow, meow, meow,
  Just like that.

- Repeat the poem using another animal and its characteristic sound.

  Creeping, creeping, creeping
  Comes the little dog.
  Woof, woof…

- Encourage your child to make the animal's sound.

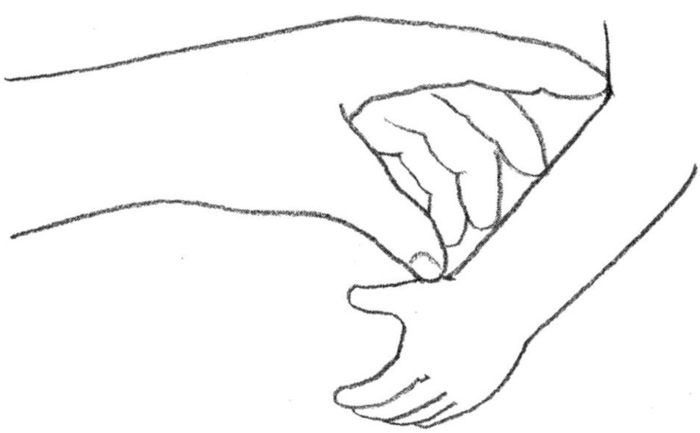

WHAT YOUR BABY WILL LEARN:
Fun

Little Mouse

- Open your baby's hand and circle your finger on her palm.
- As you move your finger, say:

  Little mouse, little mouse goes around.
  Little mouse, little mouse goes to town.

- Walk your finger up the baby's arm and tickle her under the chin.
- Try playing this game with her toes. When the mouse goes to town, walk your finger up the baby's leg to her tummy.

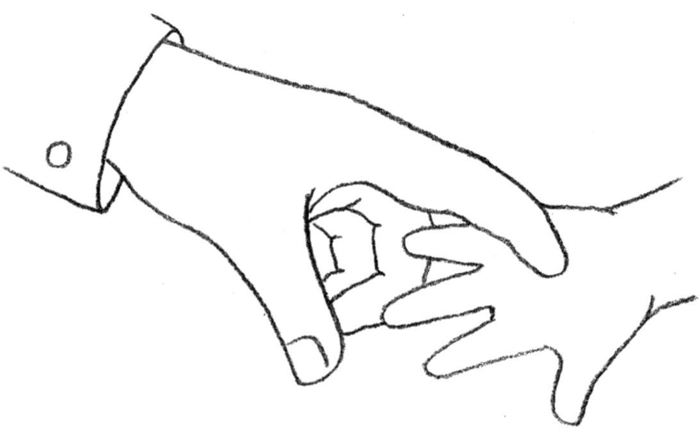

WHAT YOUR BABY WILL LEARN:
About Shapes

Circles and Music

- Sit with your baby in your lap facing you.
- Take one of her hands and move it around in a circular motion.
- Take her other hand and do the same thing.
- As you move her hands in a circle, say the word "circle."
- Now move both of her hands at the same time.
- Make circles high in the air, sideways, down low, and so on.
- Play classical music and make the circles as you listen to the music with your baby.

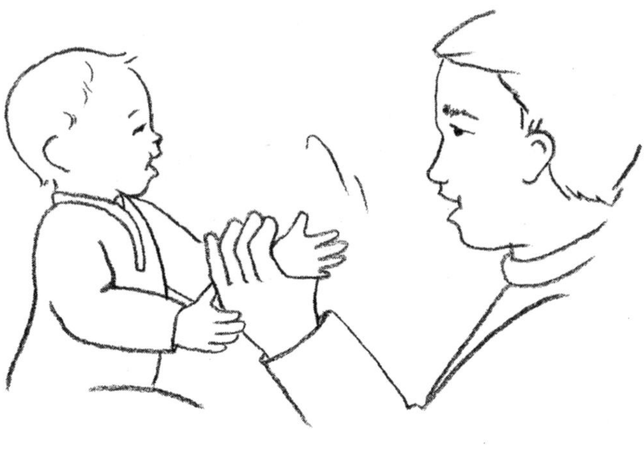

6–9 months

WHAT YOUR BABY WILL LEARN:
Relaxation

Baby Massage

- One of the most rewarding ways to bond with your baby is through massage.
- Like adults, babies collect tension in their bodies, which they often release by crying. Massage can release tension and help babies fall asleep.
- Rub some baby oil on your hands and slowly and gently massage your baby's chest and shoulders, arms and hands, hips, legs, and feet.
- Continue massaging her back.
- As you massage the baby, sing a lullaby or say loving words.

6–9 months

WHAT YOUR BABY WILL LEARN:
Fun

Where's the Mousie?

- Hold your baby with her head over your shoulder.
- Starting at the baby's waist, walk your fingers up her back to her shoulder, and tickle her under the neck.
- As you walk your fingers up her back, say:

  Mousie, mousie, where's the mousie?

- When you reach the baby's shoulder, and you're ready to tickle her under the neck, say:

  Here's the mousie, BOO!

- Turn the baby over and hold her in your lap. Play the same game starting at her tummy.

WHAT YOUR BABY WILL LEARN:
Relaxation

Stretch Up High

- This is a nice way to relax your baby before bedtime.
- Sit on the floor with your baby facing you. First recite the rhyme and act out the movement yourself. Repeat it a second time with the baby.

Stretch up high as tall as a house, (Stretch your hands up high.)
Curl up small, as small as a mouse. (Curl up small.)
Now pretend you're very sleepy, (Yawn.)
Let your whole body get sleepy. (Flop like a rag doll.)
Flop your hands and flop your feet, (Flop your hands and feet.)
Close your eyes and go to sleep. (Pretend to sleep.)

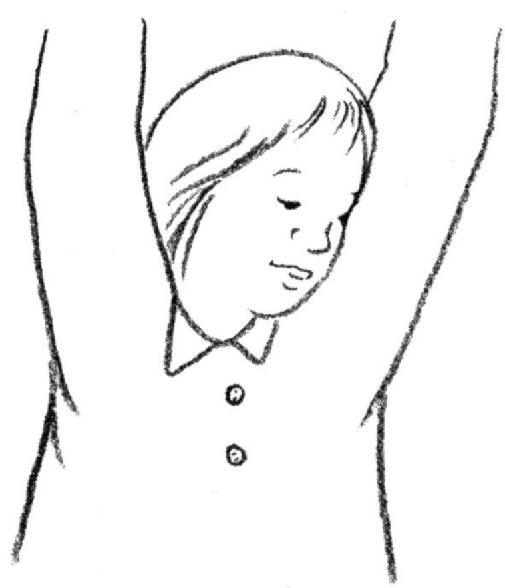

WHAT YOUR BABY WILL LEARN:
Exercise

One, Two, Kick!

- Lie on the floor next to your baby.
- Put a small blanket over your feet, then kick it off.
- When you kick off the blanket, recite this poem.

One, two, kick it off,
Kick it off, kick it off.
One, two, kick it off,
Kick it off my darling.

- You can also sing this poem to the tune of "Skip to My Lou."
- Lay the baby on the floor and put the blanket over her feet. Sing the song and help her kick off the blanket.

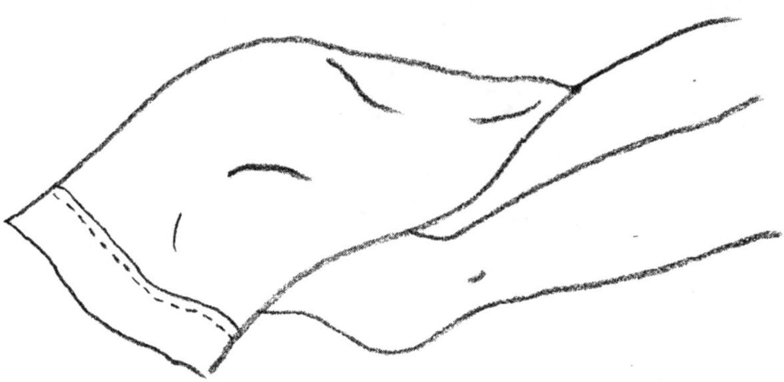

WHAT YOUR BABY WILL LEARN:
Exercise

Ball Rolls

- A large beach ball can be a wonderful tool for exercising your baby and for having fun.
- Put your baby on her tummy on top of a beach ball.
- Holding the baby firmly, roll the ball back and forth. ***NOTE***: Always hold the baby while she is on top of the ball.
- Recite this poem as you roll the ball.

  Roll the ball, roll the ball,
  Back and forth, back and forth,
  Roll the ball, roll the ball,
  One, two, whooooo!

- On the word "whoooo!" kiss the baby on her back.

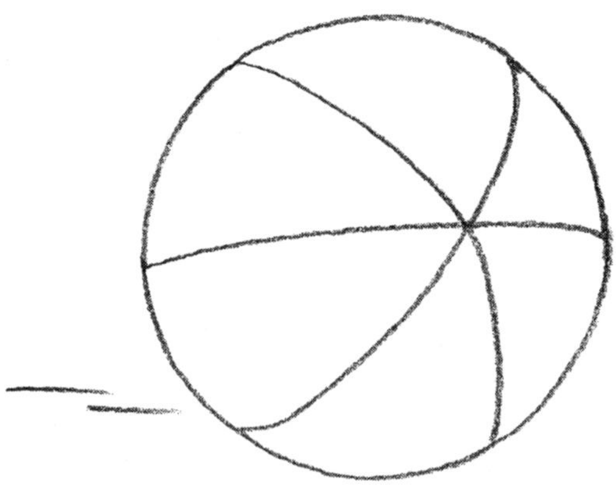

6–9 months

WHAT YOUR BABY WILL LEARN:
Exercise

Bend and Stretch

- Lay your baby on her back on a flat, padded surface. Hold her feet and gently raise them near her face and say, "Bend and stretch, bend and stretch."
- Gently touch the baby's right foot to her left foot. Then gently touch her left foot to her right foot. Each time, say, "Bend and stretch, bend and stretch."
- Cross the baby's arms in and out over her chest, saying, "Bend and stretch, bend and stretch."
- Let the baby grasp your index fingers. Raise her arms up and down while saying, "Bend and stretch, bend and stretch."
- Finally, while firmly holding the baby's hands, lift her to a sitting position, then gently move her back down, saying, "Bend and stretch, bend and stretch."
- Eventually the baby will pull up to a standing position. She will love every minute of this exercise.

WHAT YOUR BABY WILL LEARN:
To Drop Objects

The Dropping Game

- You will need a small ball and an empty coffee can for this game. ***NOTE***: Be sure that the coffee can has no sharp edges.
- Sit the baby on the floor and place the coffee can in front of her.
- Place the ball in the baby's hand and hold it over the can. Open her fingers to let the ball drop into the can.
- When you hear the ball hit the bottom of the can, say, "Boom."
- Repeat this several times, and soon the baby will drop the ball all by herself.
- You may need to help the baby retrieve the ball.

6–9 months

WHAT YOUR BABY WILL LEARN:
Coordination

Crawling Fun

- Set up objects for your baby to crawl over, under, and around to help her learn more about the world.
- Pile a group of pillows on the floor for her to crawl over.
- Put her beside a table that she can crawl under.
- Let her chase you around a chair.
- Crawl backwards and see whether she can imitate you.
- Place a toy on a low chair to encourage her to crawl to the chair and reach for the toy.

WHAT YOUR BABY WILL LEARN:
Coordination

Floor Games

- Get down on the floor with your baby and crawl around. See if you can persuade her to crawl with you.
- Pretend to be a dog or a cat and say, "Woof, woof" or "Meow, meow."
- Fill a laundry basket with toys and put it on the floor. Encourage the baby to take a toy out of the basket and then put it back.
- When the baby takes a toy out of the basket, name the toy.

WHAT YOUR BABY WILL LEARN:
Cooperation

Tug of War

- Get on the floor with your baby.
- Give her one end of a long sock while you grasp the other end.
- Gently pull the sock toward you.
- Show the baby how to pull the end toward herself.
- Pretend the baby is so strong that she pulls you over.

6–9 months

WHAT YOUR BABY WILL LEARN:
Hand-Eye Coordination

The Floating Game

- Gather together diapers, scarves, cloth belts, and other soft materials that will float in the air.
- Sit on the floor with your baby.
- Throw the first item into the air. (Scarves are a good item to begin with.) As it floats back down, extend your arms to catch it.
- Throw the scarf into the air again and tell the baby to catch it. Hold her arms out so that the scarf falls into her arms.
- Continue playing with different items. The baby will soon try to catch them herself.

WHAT YOUR BABY WILL LEARN:
Exploration Skills

Exploring Game

- Find a grassy area with plenty of room for the baby to crawl.
- Sit on the grass with the baby in your lap. Pick up a blade of grass and tickle the baby's nose with it, saying, "Grass."
- Crawl around in the grass with your baby.
- Play hide-and-seek behind a chair or a bush. See whether she can find you.
- Put some of the baby's favorite toys in the grass. Put them in interesting places so that when she crawls to them, she explores different surroundings.

6–9 months

WHAT YOUR BABY WILL LEARN:
Dexterity

Three Blocks, Two Hands

- This activity helps to develop the baby's hand release skills, which is a very important development.
- Put your baby in a high chair or on the floor.
- Place two blocks in front of the baby.
- If the baby doesn't pick up the blocks, put them in her hand.
- Take a third block and give it to the baby. She will learn to drop one block so that she can pick up another.

WHAT YOUR BABY WILL LEARN:
Language Skills

What Toy Is It?

- Sit your baby in a high chair.
- Pick out three of her favorite toys that have one-word names. For example, choose a ball, a doll, and a block.
- Pick up the ball and say, "Ball."
- Pick up the doll and say, "Doll."
- Pick up the block and say, "Block."
- Ask your baby to pick up the ball. Next, ask her to pick up the doll, and then the block.
- You may have to do this several times before the baby associates the words with the objects.

WHAT YOUR BABY WILL LEARN:
To Drink from a Cup

Cup Games

- Sit your baby in a high chair or in front of a flat surface that she can reach.
- Set a small cup in front of her.
- Pick up the cup and pretend to drink from it, saying words like "yum, yum" or "good, good."
- Hold the cup to the baby's mouth and say the same words as she pretends to drink.
- Place the cup on the tray. See whether the baby will play the game by herself.

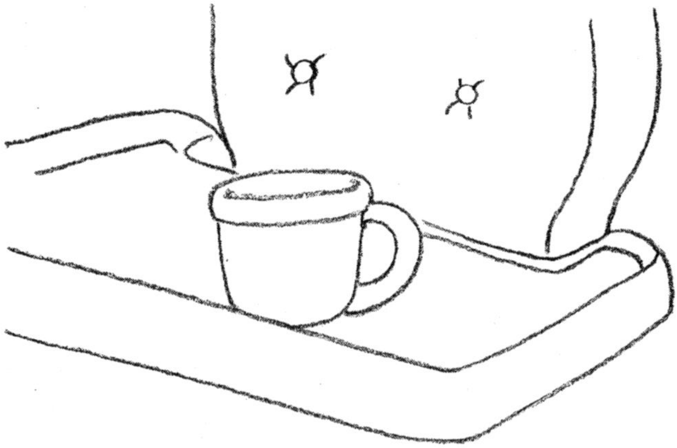

6–9 months

WHAT YOUR BABY WILL LEARN:
To Pick Up Small Objects

The Cracker Game

- Take a bite out of a cracker. Give your baby a bite.
- Break the cracker into small pieces and pick up one piece to eat. Encourage your baby to do the same.
- Drop a piece of cracker into the bottom part of a film canister or an unbreakable jar. Turn it upside down and shake out the cracker.
- Again, drop a piece of cracker into the film canister, and see if your baby can shake it out.
- Place several pieces of cracker into the canister. This time snap on the lid. Let your baby try taking off the lid to retrieve the crackers.

6–9 months

WHAT YOUR BABY WILL LEARN:
Creativity

The Macaroni Game

- Cook macaroni and place a few strands on the high chair tray.
- Show the baby how to move it around. Pick it up, shake it, and talk about its texture.
- Let the baby experiment. Encourage all of her actions.
- Stick several pieces of the macaroni together and let the baby attempt to take them apart.

WHAT YOUR BABY WILL LEARN:
Fun

Muffin Tin Game

- Place a toy into one of the cups of a small muffin tin.
- Show the baby how to take out the toy and put it back.
- Encourage the baby to take out the toy and put it back.
- Put another toy into a second cup and repeat the activity.
- Keep adding toys until you have filled all the muffin cups.
- Your baby will get endless enjoyment out of taking out the toys and putting them back.

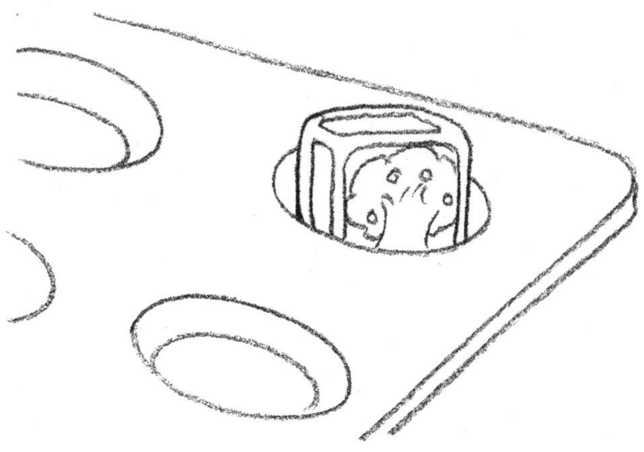

WHAT YOUR BABY WILL LEARN:
About Sounds

The Spoon Game

- Babies love to bang spoons on surfaces or against another spoon.
- Give your baby a wooden spoon and show her how to hit it on different surfaces—the table, floor, newspaper, and so on.
- Give your baby two metal spoons and show her how to bang them together, as well as on different surfaces.
- Ask her, “Can you make the spoons go bang?” When she does it, shout, “Yeahhhhh!”
- Give the baby a pot and show her how to stir the spoon in the pot. This takes a lot of hand-eye coordination.

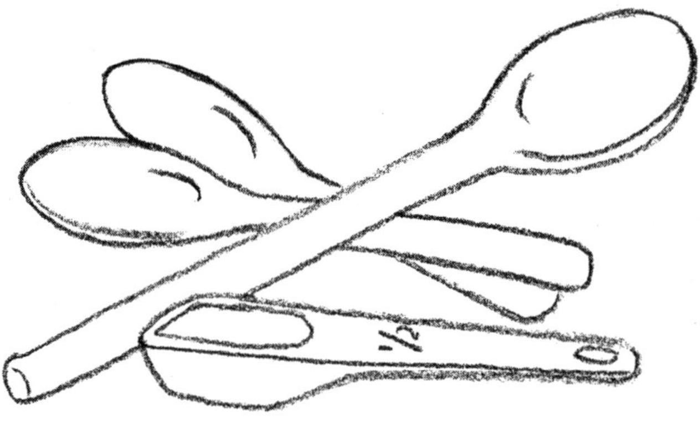

WHAT YOUR BABY WILL LEARN:
Problem-Solving Skills

Pots and Pans

- Babies love to play with pots and pans.
- Show the baby how to put a lid on a pot.
- After the baby can put on the lid without any problem, add a second lid of a different size.
- See if the baby can solve the problem of which lid to put on the pot.
- Put small toys or edible food inside the pot. When the baby takes off the lid, she will find a surprise.

6–9 months

WHAT YOUR BABY WILL LEARN:
To Manipulate Small Objects

Fast-Food Fun

- Taking a baby to a fast-food restaurant can be a wonderful learning experience for her. She will encounter many new sights and sounds.
- You can make a simple toy for her to play with in the high chair.
- Take the lids from several drinking cups and put them onto one straw, leaving space between each lid.
- Show the baby how to take the lids off and put them on again.
- Let the baby try it by herself.

WHAT YOUR BABY WILL LEARN:
Fun

The Dancing Game

- Tie a short piece of ribbon to the head of a small stuffed toy or a rag doll.
- Show the baby how you can hold and tug the ribbon to make the doll dance up and down.
- As you make the doll dance, move it side to side, back and forth, and up and down.
- As you move the doll, sing your favorite song, hum a tune, or make up a song.
- Your baby will enjoy this game very much and will want to try to make the doll dance, too.

WHAT YOUR BABY WILL LEARN:
About Sounds

The Paper Game

- Collect various kinds of paper—wrapping paper, aluminum foil, tissue paper, and so on.
- Crumple a piece of paper in your hand.
- Give the same kind of paper to the baby and help her crumple it in her hand.
- Select a different kind of paper and crinkle it in your hand.
- Give this kind of paper to your baby and let her crinkle it, too.
- Crumple the paper and drop it into a paper sack.
- Encourage your baby to copy you.
- The baby will enjoy not only the various crinkling sounds, but also dropping the crumpled-up paper into a sack.

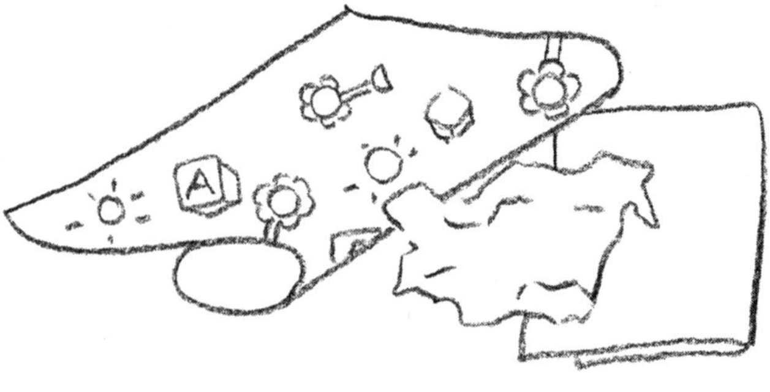

WHAT YOUR BABY WILL LEARN:
About Textures

Feels Good

- Hold the baby in your arms and take a texture walk through the house.
- Let your baby feel objects as you name their texture.
- Find and describe objects that are rough, slick, smooth, soft, hard, prickly, silky, bumpy, and cool. Examples are:

Carpet—soft
Refrigerator—cool
Floor—hard
Stuffed toy—smooth
Scarf—silky

6–9 months

WHAT YOUR BABY WILL LEARN:
About Textures

Touch This

- Find a quiet place where you and your baby can play together without interruption.
- Collect items that have a variety of textures. For example, collect foil, cotton balls, emery boards, corduroy, velvet, satin, wool, wax paper, and cork.
- Glue several items onto a large piece of cardboard.
- Place the baby's hand on each item and tell her what she is touching. Make comments like, "smooth," "nice," "soft," and "cool."
- This game is also excellent for language development.

6–9 months

WHAT YOUR BABY WILL LEARN:
Exploration Skills

Texture Crawl

- Find articles that have interesting textures, such as a rubber floor mat, throw rug, carpet sample, soft blanket, silk scarf, or scrap of velvet.
- Place the articles on the floor and, with your baby, crawl over them one at a time.
- As you crawl over the objects, describe their textures using words such as smooth, bumpy, cool, and so on.
- When you have done this many times, rearrange the articles in a different order.

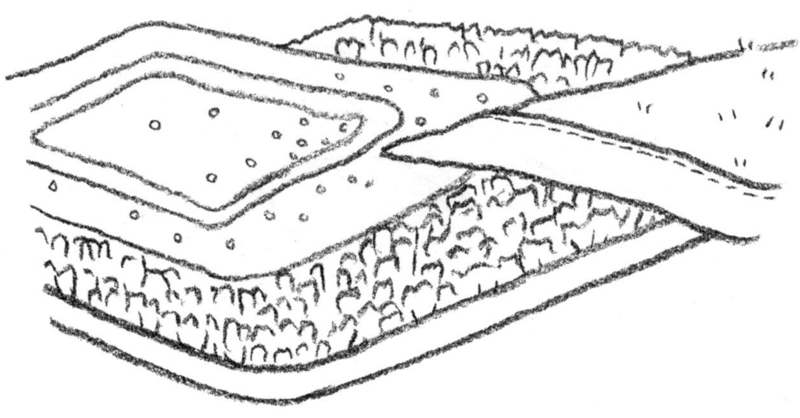

6–9 months

WHAT YOUR BABY WILL LEARN:
Cognitive Thinking

What Happens Next

- Babies at this age begin to understand cause and effect. A classic example is turning a light switch on and off.
- Turn on a switch and show your baby that when you turn on the switch, the light goes on.
- Take her hand and put it on the switch. Holding her hand, help her turn on the switch.
- Tell her what she did and what happened. "You turned on the switch and the light went on." Keep the tone of your voice upbeat.
- Find another light switch and repeat the same action.

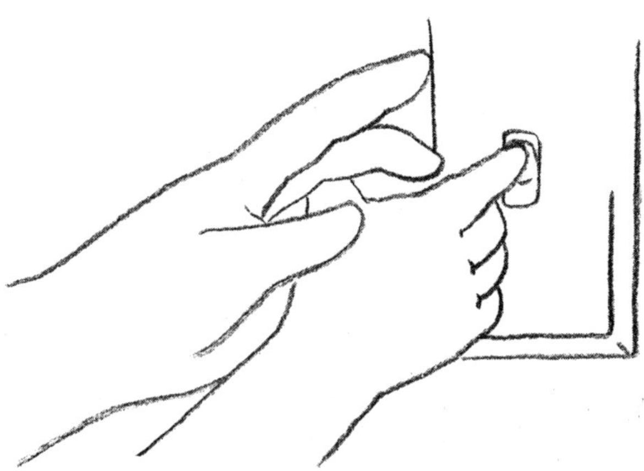

6–9 months

WHAT YOUR BABY WILL LEARN:
Observation Skills

Where's the Doll?

- When a baby looks at herself in the mirror, she doesn't realize that she is seeing her own image.
- Hold your baby's favorite doll or stuffed toy and make it move around. Pretend that it is talking.
- Now hold the doll in front of a mirror and move it around in the same way. Ask the baby, "Where's the doll?"

WHAT YOUR BABY WILL LEARN:
Attentive Listening

Sound vs. Silence

- Silence is an important part of auditory discrimination.
- When a room is quiet, you are able to concentrate on the sounds around you.
- When there is constant background music or noise, you can't hear other things in the environment.
- Hold your baby in your arms as you play some music.
- Dance around the room to the music.
- Turn off the music, stop dancing, and hold her quietly.
- Repeat this activity several times so that she will begin to understand the difference between sound and silence.

WHAT YOUR BABY WILL LEARN:
Listening Skills

Familiar Sounds

- Help the baby become aware of different sounds in her environment.
- Each time you want to call attention to a particular sound, name it for her. For example, name the sound of the telephone, footsteps, running water, doorbell, television, and so on. If possible, point to the source of the sound when you name it.
- Take your baby outside and identify the sounds that you hear. Listen for birds, airplanes, children playing, and so on. Again, if it is possible, point to the source of the sound as you name it. This helps focus the baby's attention.
- You can also ask the baby a question: "Did you hear the telephone?" Then pick up the telephone and say, "This is the telephone."

6–9 months

WHAT YOUR BABY WILL LEARN:
Language Skills

Choo, Choo, Choo, Happy Game

- When you repeat the same word many times and then say a new word, your baby will pay attention to the new word. This is called "shaping."
- Hold your baby in your lap facing you.
- Say the words "choo, choo" as you bounce the baby up and down on your knees. Say the words several times and then say a different word. For example, "Choo, choo, choo, choo, happy."
- Do this several times so that the baby becomes familiar with the new word.
- Now, use the word "happy" in several sentences. "I'm a happy mom" or "Here's a happy face."
- Your baby will become familiar with the word "happy " and will recognize it when she hears it.
- The more words that your baby hears, the more words she will understand.

6–9 months

WHAT YOUR BABY WILL LEARN:
Language Skills

Mama, Dada

- At this age, babies begin to associate language with people and things.
- Arrange large photographs of Mommy, Daddy, and other relatives the baby knows next to the crib, high chair, and changing area.
- When the baby starts making sounds like "dada," point to the picture of Daddy and say, "This is Daddy."
- Point to the pictures at other times and use the person's name in a sentence. "Mommy loves you," "Grandma is coming today," and so on.

WHAT YOUR BABY WILL LEARN:
Language Skills

Name the Clothes

- Dressing your baby is a wonderful opportunity to develop her language skills.
- Put the baby's clothes on the bed.
- Hold her in your arms and as you pick up each item of clothing (such as shoes, socks, and a shirt), say its name.
- Say, "Where is the shoe?"
- If the baby points to the shoe, praise her.
- If she doesn't indicate where the shoe is, pick it up, and tell her its name again.
- Put the shoe on her foot and say, "Here is the shoe."

6–9 months

WHAT YOUR BABY WILL LEARN:
Cognitive Thinking

Using Signs with Words

- Observe your infant carefully and identify her favorite activities. For example, the word "eat" is important to infants.
- As you say the word "eat," make a sign with your hand. For exmple, put your hand to your lips.
- Each time you say the word "eat," put your hand to your mouth to reinforce the meaning of the word.
- Your baby will learn to recognize the word by the sound and the sign.
- Other easy words to make signs for are "wash," "more," "up," "down," "love," and "sleep."
- Babies need to hear a word used in context about 200 times before they fully understand it and eventually use it.

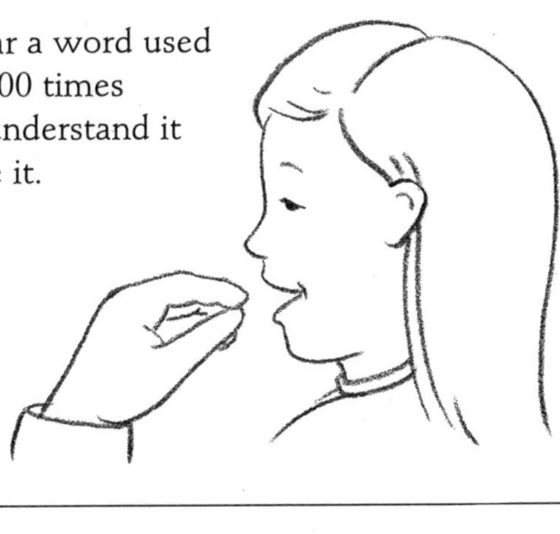

6–9 months

WHAT YOUR BABY WILL LEARN:
Self-Esteem

The Baby Story

- Your baby will love hearing her name in a story.
- Find books or magazines that have pictures of babies in them.
- Point to a baby and call her by the same name as your baby.
- Make up a story using your baby's name.

> *Once upon a time there was a little baby named Timmy (use your child's name). Timmy could touch his toes. Can you touch your toes? Timmy could clap his hands. Can you clap your hands?*

- Let the story last as long as your baby will pay attention.

6–9 months

WHAT YOUR BABY WILL LEARN:
Language Skills

Telephone Talk

- This is a wonderful game to develop language skills.
- Get a toy telephone or unplug a real one.
- Sit the baby on your lap and hold the phone to your ear as you talk. Say a short sentence: "Hello, __________ (child's name)."
- Hold the phone to the baby's ear and repeat the same sentence.
- After you have done this a few times, pretend to have a longer conversation (two or three sentences). Use the baby's name and other words that she understands like "daddy" and "bye-bye" in the conversation.
- Next, put the phone to the baby's ear, and see whether she will talk into it.

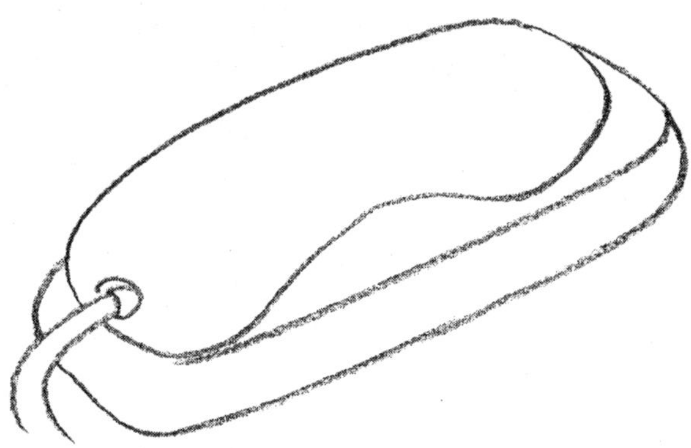

6–9 months

WHAT YOUR BABY WILL LEARN:
Language Skills

Loo Loo Loo

- Singing songs that repeat the same syllable is a wonderful way to develop your child's language skills.
- Babies will imitate and practice a repeated sound.
- Lullabies traditionally include the sound "loo."
- Think of familiar lullabies, and as you rock your baby, sing the melody using only the sound "loo."
- Lullabies include "Hush Little Baby," "Hush-A-Bye," and "Brahm's Lullaby" ("Lullaby and Good Night"). Try and remember the songs that were sung to you as a child.

6–9 months

WHAT YOUR BABY WILL LEARN:
To Shake an Object

Bang It and Shake It

- Play this game when the baby is alert.
- Sit the baby in a high chair or on an uncarpeted floor.
- Bang a block on the table or floor to attract the baby's attention. Encourage the baby to do the same, and express your delight at her attempt.
- Repeat this activity by shaking a rattle.
- Once the baby gets the idea of holding onto an object while shaking or banging it, try singing a song along with her.
- A nursery rhyme like "Mary Had a Little Lamb" or "The Farmer in the Dell" works very well.

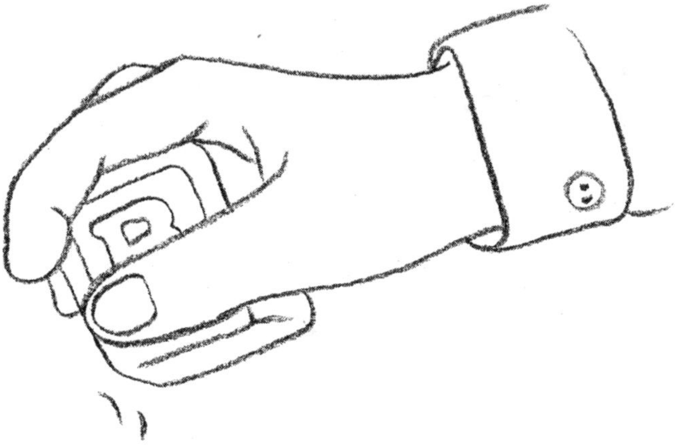

WHAT YOUR BABY WILL LEARN:
Rhythm

Making Music

- Take out a pie pan and a spoon. Hit the spoon on the pie pan a few times.
- Give the baby the pie pan and spoon. Help her hit the spoon on the pie pan.
- As the baby hits the pie pan, sing a familiar song like "Row, Row, Row Your Boat" or "Mary Had a Little Lamb."
- As the baby hits the pie pan, clap your hands and sing.
- Babies really love this game, and you will find that your baby will often play it by herself.

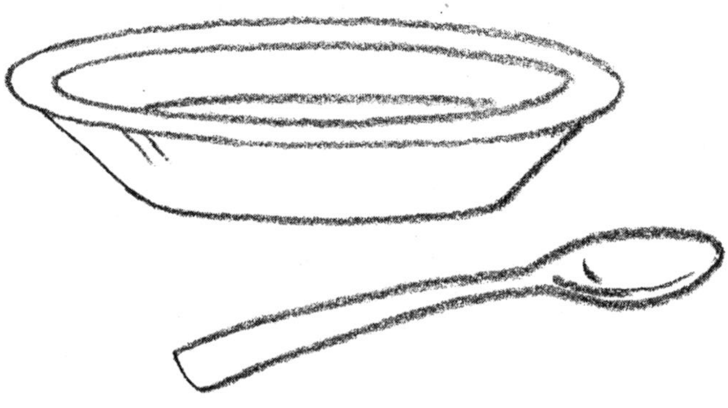

WHAT YOUR BABY WILL LEARN:
About Sounds

Music Listening

- Listening to music can be a wonderful stimulant, as well as a very relaxing experience.
- Play different kinds of music for your baby.
- Hold the baby and dance around to fast music.
- Rock the baby gently to soft, slow music such as ballet music. (*Swan Lake* is a good choice.)
- March with the baby to music with a strong marching beat, such as pieces by John Phillips Sousa.
- Bounce the baby on your lap to bouncy, exuberant music.

WHAT YOUR BABY WILL LEARN:
Language Skills

Old MacDonald

- Get a set of plastic animals.
- Hold up each animal for the baby to see, then say the animal's name and make its characteristic sound.
- Give the baby each animal after you say its name, and let her feel it. While the baby is holding the animal, repeat its name and the sound it makes.
- Sing the song "Old MacDonald Had a Farm."
- As you sing each verse, pick up the animal that is named and move it around.

6–9 months

WHAT YOUR BABY WILL LEARN:
Thinking Skills

Song Cues

- Pick three songs that you and your baby enjoy singing together. "Twinkle, Twinkle Little Star," "Old MacDonald Had a Farm," and "Mary Had a Little Lamb" are three popular songs.
- Try associating one of the songs with one of the baby's regular activities. For example, sing "Twinkle, Twinkle Little Star" each night when it's time to get the baby ready for bed.
- Choose a different song for when it's time to take a bath, eat, or go outside.
- Each time your baby hears a certain song, she will know what activity is coming next.
- If she hears one of the song cues when she is in a different environment, such as at Grandma's house, she will not expect the usual activity to follow. For example, she will not expect to take a bath while she is riding in a car.
- Routines and rituals are reassuring to babies. They help babies learn what to expect and how to understand the world around them.

6–9 months

WHAT YOUR BABY WILL LEARN:
Listening Skills

One, Two, One, Two

- Play instrumental music. Holding your baby, sway back and forth as you dance around the room.
- Show the baby different ways to move with the music. Clapping hands, stomping feet, and swinging arms are a few ideas.
- Play vocal music. Pick out a particular word in the song and sing it to the baby each time you hear it.
- You will be amazed at how quickly the baby will anticipate the word.
- Play music that is loud and soft, fast and slow, and features high and low sounds.

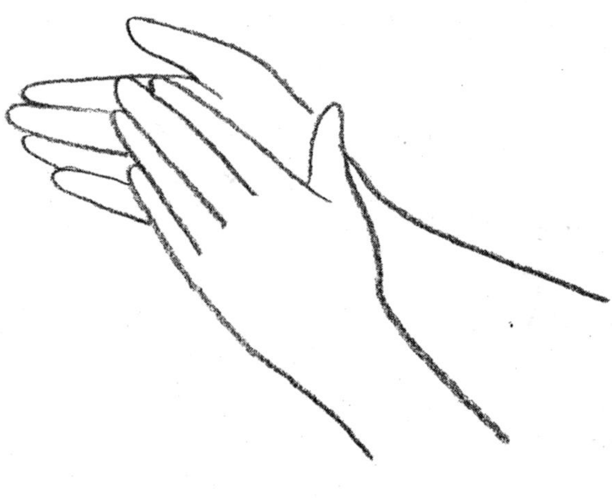

9–12 months

WHAT YOUR BABY WILL LEARN:
Bonding

Sleep Song

- Bedtime is a good time to sing to your baby.
- Slowly and softly sing this song to the tune of "Good Night, Ladies."

Good night, baby, (Insert your child's name.)
Good night, baby,
Good night, baby,
It's time to go to sleep.

Sleep tight, baby,
Sleep tight, baby,
Sleep tight, baby,
Time to close your eyes.

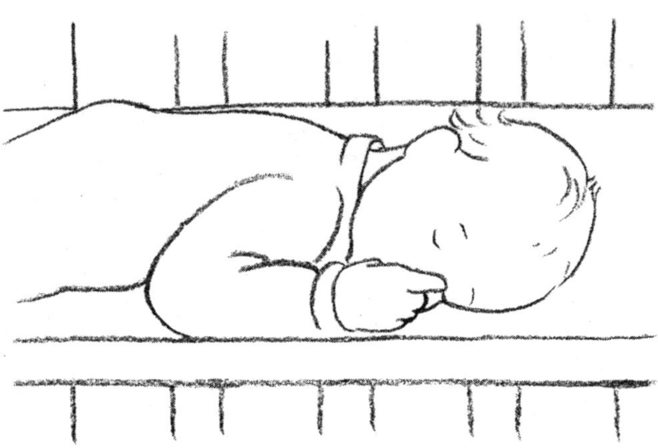

WHAT YOUR BABY WILL LEARN:
Language Skills

Niño Querido

- Rock and cuddle the baby in your arms, especially at bedtime.
- This is a lovely lullaby to sing just before bedtime. If you don't know the melody, make up your own. What's important are the words and feelings that the song conveys.

Niño querido, (neen-yoh kay-ree-tho)
Duermete ya (dwear-may-tay yah)
Que mientras tanto (kay myen-trahs tahn-toh)
Te canta mama. (tay kahn-tah mah-mah)
Niño querido, (neen-yoh kay-ree-tho)
Duermete ya. (dwear-may-tay yah)
Baby beloved, sleeping there
While Mother sings to her baby fair.
Baby beloved, sleeping there.

WHAT YOUR BABY WILL LEARN:
Language Skills

Newcastle Lullaby

- This is called a dandling song rather than a lullaby. A dandling song is sung while the baby eats and plays, before he is put in the cradle.
- You can speak or sing dandling songs. The sound of the language will be lovely for your baby to hear.
- The words are Scottish in origin, and the song comes from Newcastle-upon-Tyne, which is near Scotland in northeast England's Northumberland County.

Sleep bonnie bairnie behind the castle
By, by!
By, by!
Thou shalt have a golden apple
By, by!
By, by!

- Rock your baby as you say the words. Hold his hands and gently move them each time you say, "By, by."

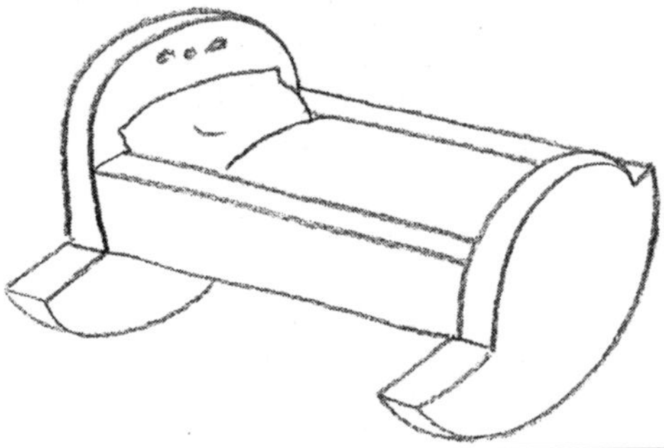

WHAT YOUR BABY WILL LEARN:
Language Skills

Sleep Story

- Make up a story to tell your baby that uses his name.
- The story should describe things that your baby does during the day.
- The following is an example.

> *Once upon a time there was a sweet little baby (your child's name). He played with his toys. Sometimes he would go outside to see the birds and the grass. At dinnertime, he drank his milk and ate his dinner.*
>
> *Every night, his mommy (or daddy) gave him a bath and lots of kisses. After his mommy (or daddy) laid him in his crib, he closed his eyes and went to sleep.*

- Use your child's name in the story as often as possible.

WHAT YOUR BABY WILL LEARN:
A Bedtime Routine

I See the Moon

- Look outside with your baby and talk about the moon and the stars.
- Tell your baby that the moon and stars help people fall asleep because they remind us that it is nighttime.
- Teach your baby this poem about the moon and the stars.

I see the moon,
And the moon sees me.
God bless the moon,
And God bless me.

I see the stars,
And the stars see me.
God bless the stars,
And God bless me.

- Ask your child what else he sees and insert those things into the poem. For example:

I see mommy,
And mommy sees me.
God bless mommy,
And God bless me.

WHAT YOUR BABY WILL LEARN:
Fun

Shoe Game

- This is a poem to recite while you put on the baby's shoes.

  Shoe the old horse.
  Shoe the old mare.
  But let the little colt
  Go bare, bare, bare.

- Recite the last line as you tie your baby's shoe. Tap the sole of the foot each time you say, "Bare, bare, bare."
- The baby will begin to look forward to the tapping.

WHAT YOUR BABY WILL LEARN:
To Follow Directions

Combing Game

- Sit your baby in your lap. Stroke his hair and say, "Soft hair."
- Put the baby's hands on your hair and say, "Daddy's hair."
- Run a comb through your baby's hair.
- Show your baby how you comb your hair.
- Find a doll with hair and run the comb through its hair.
- Give the doll to your baby and ask him to comb the doll's hair.
- Ask the baby to comb his own hair.
- Ask the baby to comb your hair.

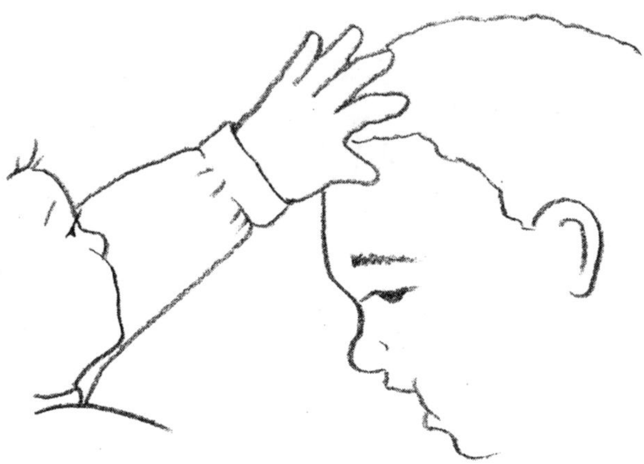

WHAT YOUR BABY WILL LEARN:
Body Awareness

Powder Puff Fun

- This is a great way to keep your baby still while you change his diaper.
- Give a large powder puff to your baby. Let him feel and explore it.
- Rub the powder puff on his tummy as you recite this rhyme.

Powder puff, powder puff,
On your tummy, on your tummy.
Powder puff, powder puff,
Tummy, tummy, boo!

- Tickle your baby on the word "boo!"
- Continue placing the puff on different parts of his body. Each time you touch a new part, name that part in the poem.

9–12 months

WHAT YOUR BABY WILL LEARN:
Fun

The Rainmaker

- Play this rainmaking game in the bathtub.
- Punch holes in a plastic bottle and give it to your baby.
- Show him how to fill the bottle with water and hold it in the air to make it rain.
- Your baby will be delighted with this activity. Sing "rain" songs such as "Rain, Rain, Go Away" and "It's Raining, It's Pouring."

9–12 months

WHAT YOUR BABY WILL LEARN:
Body Awareness

The Washing Game

- This game is best to play at bath time. Tightly wring out a washcloth and give it to your baby.
- Make up your own melody and sing the words, "Can you wash your face?" Take the baby's hand and rub the washcloth gently on his face, and sing, "Yes, I can, yes, I can."
- Continue playing this game as you name all the parts of his body: hands, feet, cheek, nose, ears, and so on.
- Next, ask him to wash his face, hands, nose, and so on.
- Play the same game as you dry the baby, using a towel instead of a washcloth.

9–12 months

WHAT YOUR BABY WILL LEARN:
Cognitive Skills

A Bath Surprise

- While your baby is in the bathtub, show him a floating toy. Let him hold it for a few minutes.
- Take the toy from your baby and place it in the water in front of her.
- Cover the toy with a washcloth and ask, "Where is the toy? Where did it go?"
- Remove the washcloth and say, "Hooray, here it is. It was hiding under the washcloth."
- Play this game several times and encourage the baby to lift the washcloth off the toy.
- If the baby doesn't understand after the first few times, guide his hands to remove the washcloth.

WHAT YOUR BABY WILL LEARN:
To Strengthen Hand Muscles

Squeeze Fun

- This is a lovely game to play at bath time.
- Fill the bathtub with several squeeze toys, sponges, and a washcloth.
- Ask the baby to squeeze one of the toys. Ask him if you may have a turn.
- When you have squeezed two or three toys, take a sponge, and squeeze it on your hand.
- Ask the baby if you may squeeze it on his hand.
- Repeat this with the washcloth. First squeeze it on your hand, then his.
- Now show the baby how to squeeze the sponge or washcloth on one of the toys.

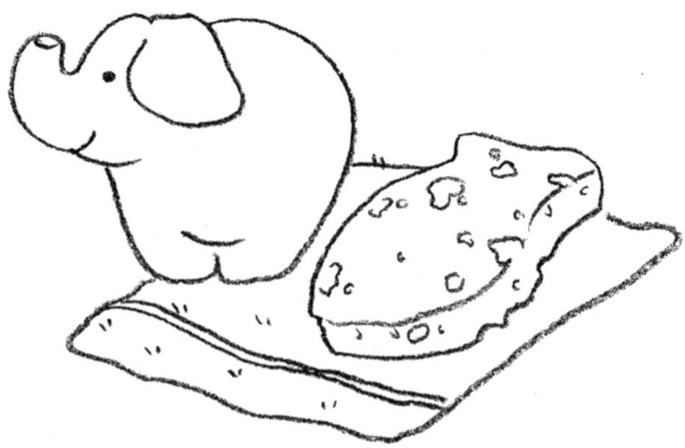

9–12 months

WHAT YOUR BABY WILL LEARN:
Hand-Eye Coordination

Floating Surprise

- Wrap a floating bath toy in a washcloth and move it around the bathtub.
- Give it to your baby and see whether he can unwrap it.
- After he unwraps the toy, squeeze the water from the washcloth over it.
- Ask your baby to squeeze the cloth over the toy.
- As the water is dripping, shout, "Whee!"
- Ask the baby to wrap the toy for you. This requires hand-eye coordination.

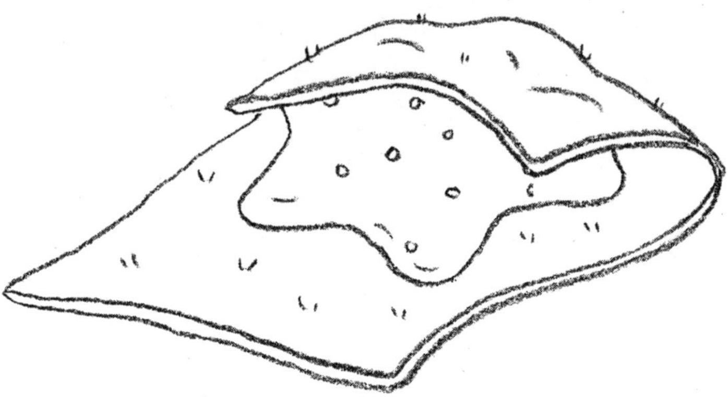

WHAT YOUR BABY WILL LEARN:
Hand-Eye Coordination

Catch the Toy

- Babies love to play in water. The baby can practice his pouring skills in or out of the tub.
- Show your baby how to scoop water with a ladle and pour it into a container.
- Give the baby a strainer to scoop the water and let him experience the difference between the strainer and the ladle.
- Place floating toys in the bathtub. Let the baby try to catch the toys in the ladle and in the strainer.
- In addition to developing hand-eye coordination, this activity also teaches babies about volume.

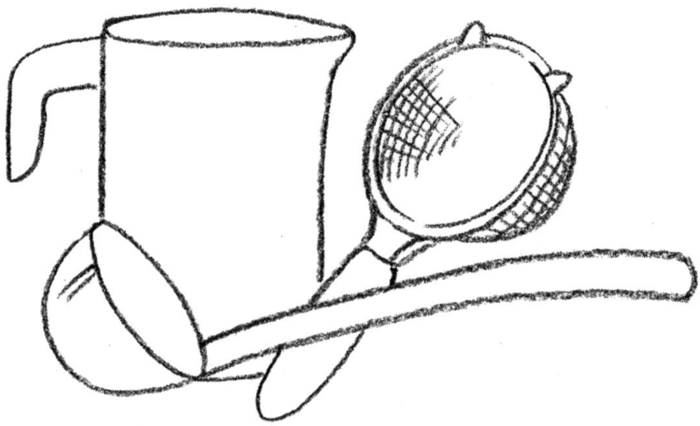

WHAT YOUR BABY WILL LEARN:
Trust

Let's Find Daddy

- If your baby gets upset when you leave the room, here are a group of games that you can play to help him adjust to the situation.
- Lie on the bed next to your baby and play peek-a-boo. Each time you say the word "peek-a-boo," hide under the blanket and then pull it back so that the baby can see your face.
- Hide somewhere in the room, such as under a table or behind a door. Say, "Where is daddy?" and then come out from hiding and say, "Here I am."
- Another game to play requires a third person. The third person should be someone your baby knows and trusts.
- Go into another room and let the third person bring the baby to you. He can say, "Let's find Daddy." Go into another room and say, "Is he here? No, let's find Daddy."
- Finally, let the baby find you after he looks in two other places.

9–12 months

WHAT YOUR BABY WILL LEARN:
Sensory Experiences

Shopping Fun

- Take your baby to the supermarket to experience many sensory experiences.
- The produce department is full of wonderful textures and smells.
- Melons have wonderful textures. Let the baby feel and smell them.
- Bananas feel interesting to little hands.
- Say the name of each fruit or vegetable that you touch or smell.
- When you return home, show the baby the fruits and vegetables that you purchased and explore the textures again.
- This time you can taste the food, too.

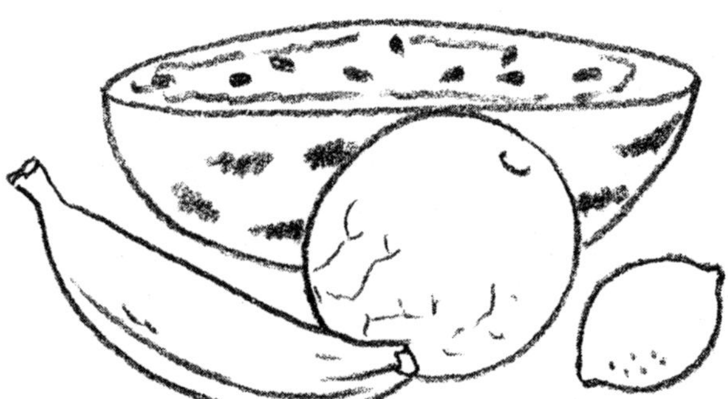

WHAT YOUR BABY WILL LEARN:
Language Skills

It's Cold

- When you take your baby to the supermarket, each time you pick up a cold item, show it to him, and let him feel it while you say the word "cold."
- When you get home, place the cold items on the counter.
- Open the refrigerator and let the baby feel inside. Tell him that it is cold.
- Hand him cold items that he can hold and ask him to put them in the refrigerator. As he does so, say, "Thank you for putting away the cold (name the item)." Name each item and use the word "cold" each time you hand him a new item.

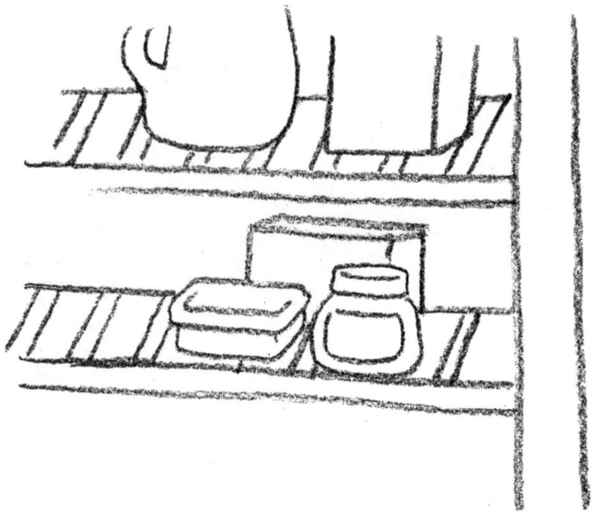

9–12 months

WHAT YOUR BABY WILL LEARN:
Safety Skills

Left, Right, Cross the Street

- Play this game when you cross the street with your baby.
- Say to the baby, "Now we are at the corner. We are going to cross the street. Let's make sure no cars are coming. Look to the left." Turn the stroller or the child to the left.
- Now say, "No cars. Okay, now let's look to the right." Turn the stroller or the child to the right.
- Next say, "No cars. Good. It's okay to cross the street."
- This game teaches the baby about traffic safety and the concept of left and right.

9–12 months

WHAT YOUR BABY WILL LEARN:
Small Motor Skills and Imagination

Wrapping with Babies

- Select three or four small toys and wrap them in tissue paper or aluminum foil.
- Show your baby one of the wrapped toys.
- Talk about the size of it.
- Ask, "What do you think is inside?"
- Give the wrapped toy to your baby and encourage him to unwrap it.
- He will be delighted to unwrap the toy.
- He may even play with it after he opens it!

WHAT YOUR BABY WILL LEARN:
Creativity

Make a Toy

- Babies always have favorite toys and containers.
- Gather a few of your baby's favorite toys and containers and string them together to make a pull toy.
- Start with two or three objects, such as a box and a stuffed animal.
- Show the baby how to pull the toy.
- Ask your baby if he wants to get more toys to pull. He will probably collect more toys.

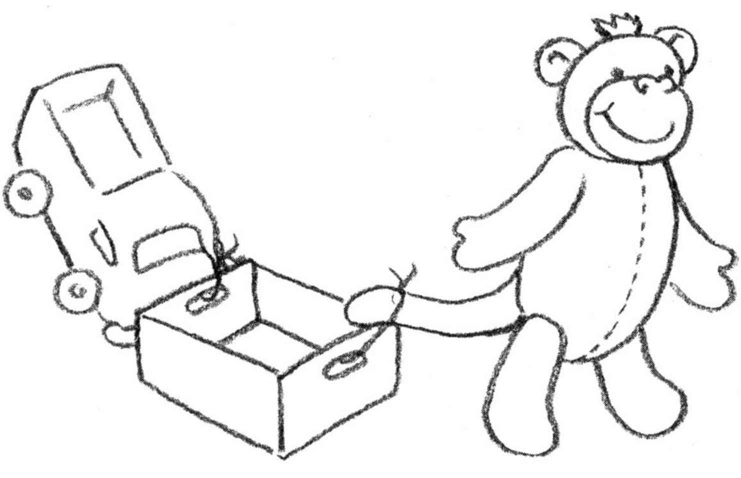

WHAT YOUR BABY WILL LEARN:
Spatial Relationships

Mr. Bear

- Say the following poem.

  Mr. Bear, Mr. Bear,
  Where can you be?
  I will find you
  Wait and see.

- Take the bear and hide it as your baby watches.
- Ask your child to find the bear.
- Describe where the bear is hidden using words like "under," "behind," "inside," and so on. "Is the bear under the table?" "Is the bear behind the chair?"
- Your baby will love finding the bear and giving it to you to hide again.
- Play this game with any stuffed animal. Just change the name.
- At this age, your baby is beginning to understand concepts of space.

WHAT YOUR BABY WILL LEARN:
Language Skills

Object Hide-and-Seek

- Sit on the floor with your baby. Sit near a hiding place like a chair or sofa.
- Show the baby a toy and let him hold it.
- Take the toy away. Say, "Now I'm going to hide the toy." While the baby is watching, hide the toy behind the couch.
- Ask the baby to find the toy. If the baby does not understand at first, retrieve the toy and try the game again.
- Keep playing this game until the baby can easily find the toy.

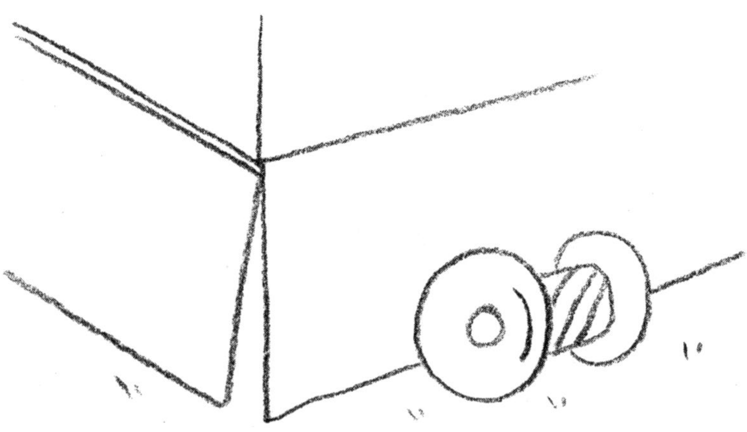

WHAT YOUR BABY WILL LEARN:
Cognitive Skills

Where Did It Go?

- This game helps your baby learn that an object still exists even if it's out of his sight.
- Sit on the floor with your baby and show him a favorite toy.
- Let the baby play with the toy for a few minutes, then ask him if you may have a turn.
- If he agrees, take the toy and cover it with a cloth. Place it within the baby's reach.
- Help him to find the toy, and then repeat the game. Ask him, "Where is the toy?" or something similar. Make a mystery out of the game.
- Play the game several times until the baby understands where the toy is and retrieves it.
- Repeat the game with a different toy or object.

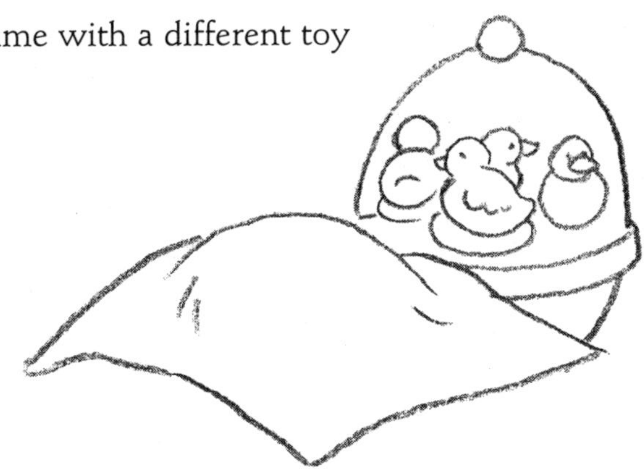

WHAT YOUR BABY WILL LEARN:
Language Skills

Give Me the Toy

- Pick three of your baby's favorite toys.
- Hold each toy in your hand and say its name.
- Put all three toys in front of your baby. Name one of the toys and ask the baby to give it to you.
- When he picks the right one, clap and praise him enthusiastically.
- Put one of the toys behind your back. Ask him where the toy is, and then bring it out from behind your back.
- Put the same toy behind the baby's back. Ask him where the toy is. Soon he will understand that the toy is behind his back.

9–12 months

WHAT YOUR BABY WILL LEARN:
To Follow Directions

Ribbon Fun

- Pick three of your baby's favorite toys and tie a short piece of ribbon around each one.
- Show the baby how to pull the ribbon to get the toy.
- Ask him to give you a toy. Put his hand on the ribbon that he needs to pull. You may have to help him at first.
- After a few tries, he will be able to pull the toy without any problem.
- Ask him to give you each toy that is tied with a ribbon.
- Try hiding a toy and leave the ribbon showing. Ask the baby where the toy is and show him how to pull the ribbon to get the toy.
- He will love doing this and laugh with great enthusiasm.

9–12 months

WHAT YOUR BABY WILL LEARN:
Exploration Skills

Gathering Treasures

- The outdoors is a wonderful place for babies to explore and discover.
- Take a bucket outside and help your baby discover rocks, leaves, branches, and twigs to put into it.
- Bring the bucket to a comfortable place and dump everything out.
- Let him hold the rocks, the leaves, and so on in his hand while you tell him the name of each treasure.
- Your baby will enjoy putting the treasures back into the bucket and dumping them out again.
- Ask him to give you a leaf or a rock.

9–12 months

WHAT YOUR BABY WILL LEARN:
Self-Esteem

Crackers

- Sit your baby in the high chair. Put crackers in front of him.
- Let him pick up a cracker and eat one.
- Put some jelly in a plastic container and put it next to the crackers.
- Give him a spoon and show him how to put the spoon into the jelly and then on the cracker.
- This activity is kind of messy, but it is worth it. Your baby will, of course, use his fingers to spread the jelly.
- Your baby will be crazy about this game.
- Encouraging your baby to do things for himself is a wonderful way to help him feel good about himself.

9–12 months

WHAT YOUR BABY WILL LEARN:
To Pick Up Small Objects

I Can Do It Myself

- Put a small piece of cereal or banana on the baby's high chair tray.
- Pick up the food and put it in your mouth, saying, "I am picking up the banana and putting it in my mouth. Yum, yum, yum."
- Take the baby's hand and help him pick up a piece of banana, saying, "(Child's name) is picking up the banana and putting it in his mouth. Yum, yum, yum."
- You may change the word at the end of the sentence from "Yum, yum, yum" to others such as "chew, chew, chew," "good, good, baby," or "oh! boy."

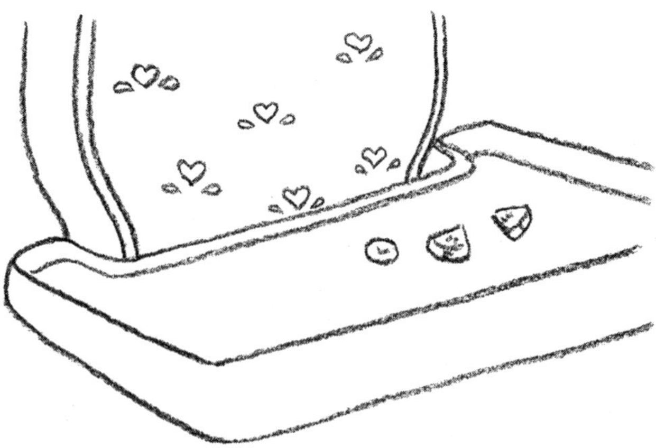

WHAT YOUR BABY WILL LEARN:
Coordination

Look, I Can Pour!

- Sit on the floor with your baby. Place paper cups filled with dry cereal in front of you. (Round oat cereal works well.)
- Show the baby how to pour the cereal from one cup to another. Then let the baby try to pour.
- Little ones will spend a lot of time doing this activity until they get it right. They will also enjoy eating what they spill.
- The next step in learning how to pour is to work with water, which will come much later.

WHAT YOUR BABY WILL LEARN:
To Use a Spoon

Water and Spoon

- This game will fascinate your baby.
- Place a fairly shallow plastic bowl and a large spoon on a table in front of your baby.
- Fill the bowl with water.
- Put an empty cup next to the bowl. Show the baby how to dip the spoon into the water and fill up the cup.
- Add pieces of ice to make it even more fun.

9–12 months

WHAT YOUR BABY WILL LEARN:
Hand-Eye Coordination

Find the Snack

- You will need three clear plastic glasses and dry cereal or small round crackers.
- Sit your baby in the high chair and while he watches, hide a cracker under one of the glasses. Let the baby find the cracker and eat it.
- Add a second glass and then a third. Always be sure your baby is watching where you hide the cracker.
- Each time the baby finds the cracker, praise him.

WHAT YOUR BABY WILL LEARN:
To Pull an Object

Choo, Choo, Food

- Tie several milk cartons together with colored yarn to make a train.
- Cut out one side of a carton and fill it with dry cereal, raisins, or other nutritious finger food.
- Show the baby how to pull the carton around on the floor.
- As you pull, say, "Choo, choo food, choo, choo food, whooo (like a train whistle), whooo."
- Say to the baby, "Let's stop at the station and have a snack." Put a raisin or piece of cereal into your mouth.
- Keep playing and encourage the baby to pull the train himself.

9–12 months

WHAT YOUR BABY WILL LEARN:
Counting

Counting Buttons

- Babies love to touch and pull on buttons. Why not take advantage of this interest and use it as a teachable moment?
- Wear a shirt that has three or more buttons.
- Say the following words as you do the actions.

  One button, one button
  Let's touch one button.
  (Put the baby's hand on one button.)
  One button, two buttons
  Let's count two buttons.
  (Touch the first button and then the second button.)

- Continue with the next button. Always touch the button as you say the number.
- The number "three" is fun for babies because many of the games you play with babies involve counting up to three.

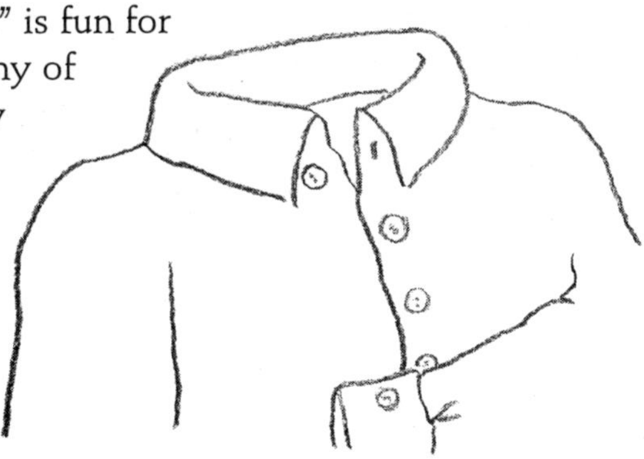

WHAT YOUR BABY WILL LEARN:
About Different Sizes

Does It Fit?

- Learning about size is a hands-on experience for babies. Touching objects and trying to fit one thing into another is the way babies learn about large and small. This happens long before they understand words like "large" and "small."
- Graduated measuring cups are excellent toys to use in teaching babies about size.
- Give your baby two cups. Put one inside the other for him to see, then let him try placing one inside the other by himself.
- When he figures out how to do this, give him a third cup.
- While he experiments with the sizes, praise him and let him know what a good job he is doing.

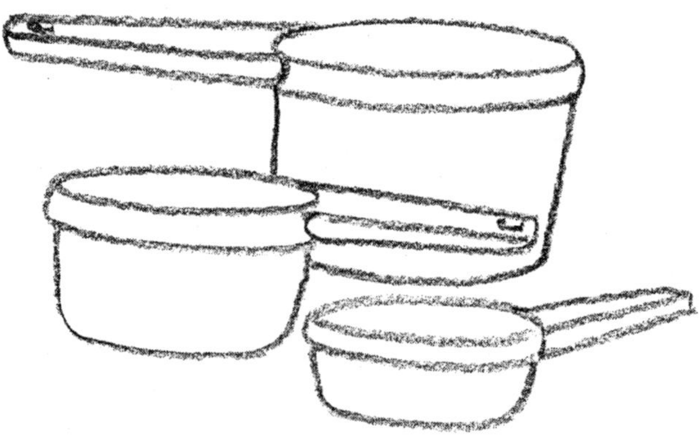

9–12 months

WHAT YOUR BABY WILL LEARN:
Coordination

Boxes, Boxes

- There are many ways to use boxes to help your baby develop his ability to use his hands.
- Find boxes with tops. Show the baby how to remove the top of a box and then put it back on. Vary the sizes and textures of the boxes.
- Boxes make great receptacles for toys, blocks, and clothespins. Show the baby how to drop things into a box and then turn it over to retrieve them. ***NOTE***: Only use objects that are too large for the baby to swallow.
- Boxes are also fun as make-believe telephones, hats, and megaphones.

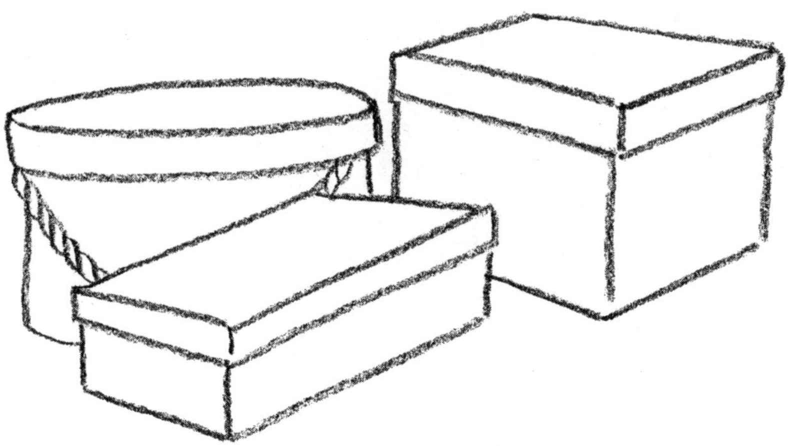

WHAT YOUR BABY WILL LEARN:
Balance

Stack Them Up

- Save containers you use in your kitchen, such as cereal boxes, margarine containers, egg cartons, milk cartons, juice cans, and plastic bottles. Be sure the containers are clean and dry, and that they have no sharp edges.
- Let your baby experiment with stacking the containers. He will learn a lot about balance.
- Show your baby how to build a tower using the containers. When it topples over, laugh with him so he understands that it's okay for it to fall down.
- Make a bridge or a tunnel with the containers and show him how to push a car across the bridge or through the tunnel.

WHAT YOUR BABY WILL LEARN:
Fun

Drop the Clothespin

- The object of this game is to drop clothespins into a container.
- You can use an empty coffee can or cut a large opening into an empty gallon milk container. ***NOTE***: Be sure the coffee can has no rough edges.
- Show the baby how to hold the clothespin to drop it into the opening. If you tilt the container at first, it will help him succeed.
- Show the baby how to turn the container upside down to remove the clothespins.

9–12 months

WHAT YOUR BABY WILL LEARN:
About Sounds and Colors

Find the Bell

- You will need three small milk cartons and contact paper for this activity.
- Cover two cartons with the same color of paper, and the third carton with a different color.
- Place a small bell or other noisemaker inside the third carton. **Securely** seal all three cartons.
- Give the baby a carton and help him shake it.
- When you give him the carton that makes noise when shaken, react to the noise so he will react as well.
- Help your baby learn to discriminate color by choosing the carton that has a sound inside.

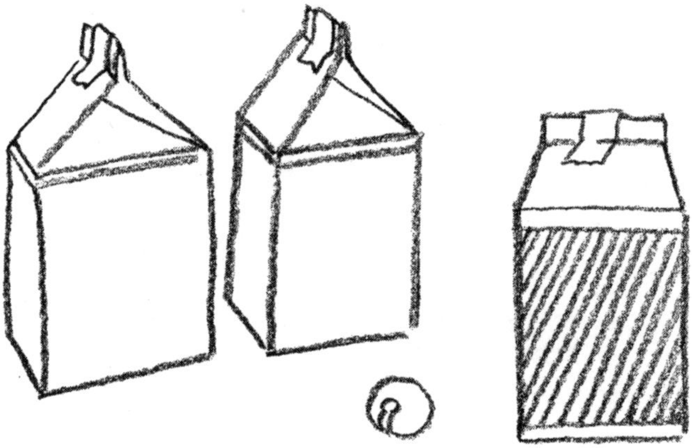

WHAT YOUR BABY WILL LEARN:
Language Skills

Hats, Hats, Hats

- Collect three different hats. Set one hat on your head and say something silly like, "Hello, silly willy."
- Place the hat on your baby's head and say the same thing.
- Repeat this game with each hat, changing your voice each time you change the hat.
- Give the hat to the baby and let him try to put it on his head.
- This is a very good game to teach your baby more about his body.
- Looking in the mirror with hats on your head is fun, too.

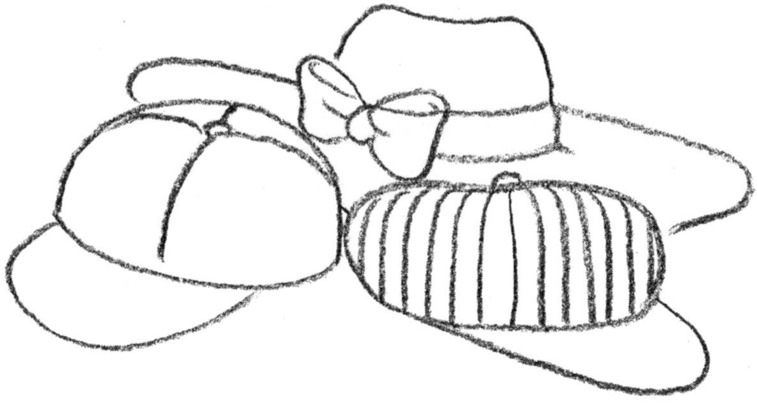

9–12 months

WHAT YOUR BABY WILL LEARN:
About Shapes and Lines

Drawing in the Snow

- Go outside with your baby on a day when there is snow on the ground.
- Show your baby how to draw a picture in the snow with his mittens.
- Try making circles, lines, and zigzags.
- Look for other drawing tools, such as sticks, rocks, and leaves.
- If you do not live in a snowy area, draw in the dirt with a stick.
- This is a highly creative game that babies adore.

9–12 months

WHAT YOUR BABY WILL LEARN:
Rhythm

Tap and Clap

- Babies like tapping on things and clapping their hands.
- Say the following poem and do the actions while sitting on the floor with your baby.

> *Tap, tap, tapping*
> (Take a spoon and hit it on the floor.)
> *Clap, clap, clapping*
> (Clap your hands together.)
> *Nap, nap, napping*
> (Lay down and pretend to sleep.)

- Repeat the poem and do the actions in a different way.
- Tap in a different place, clap with your arms in the air, and nap in a different position.
- Continue making up different ideas for each action.

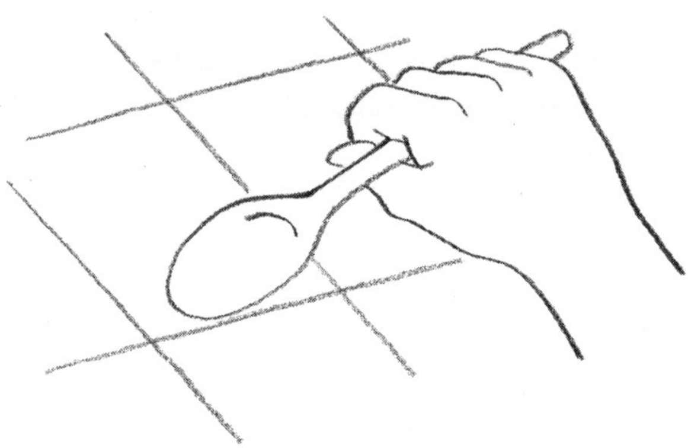

9–12 months

WHAT YOUR BABY WILL LEARN:
Coordination

Through the Hole

- Put your thumb and index finger together to make a circle.
- Point one finger on your other hand and put it through the circle. Say "BOO!"
- Recite the rhyme, wiggling your finger.

Wiggle your finger, one and two,
Wiggle your finger, one and two,
Wiggle your finger, one and two,
Through the hole and BOO!!

- On "BOO!" point your finger through the circle and shake it.
- Now let your baby play the game and push his finger through the circle. When you say, "BOO," kiss the baby's finger.
- Try to teach your baby how to make the circle with his thumb and finger. Put your finger through the circle.

WHAT YOUR BABY WILL LEARN:
Language Skills

Whoops, Johnny

- Take your baby's hand in yours.
- Starting with his pinky, touch each of his fingers with your index finger and say the word "Johnny." Keep saying "Johnny" until you reach his index finger.
- Slide your finger down his index finger and up his thumb, saying, "Whoops." When you reach the tip of the thumb, say, "Johnny."
- It will sound like this:

Johnny, Johnny, Johnny, Johnny,
Whoops Johnny,
Whoops Johnny,
Johnny, Johnny, Johnny.

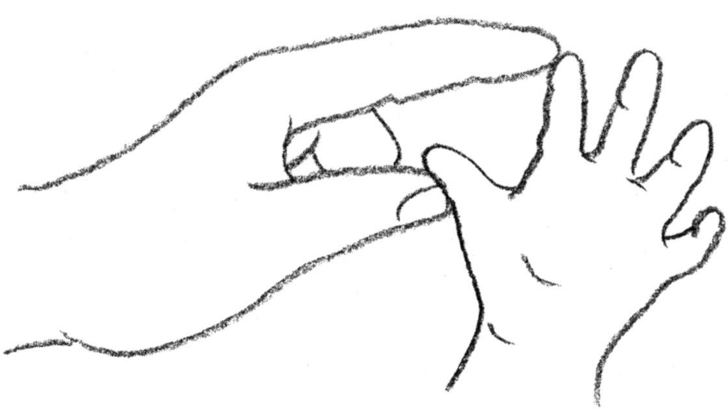

WHAT YOUR BABY WILL LEARN:
To Sit Up

So-o-o Big

- Play this game while the baby is lying on his back on a flat surface.
- Reach out to grasp your baby's fingers. Gently raise the baby to a sitting position and say, "(Insert baby's name) is so-o-o big!"
- If the baby cannot hold onto your hands, place them over his fingers.
- As the baby grows older, say, "Up so-o-o high and down we go," as you gently raise the baby up and then support him as he lies back down.

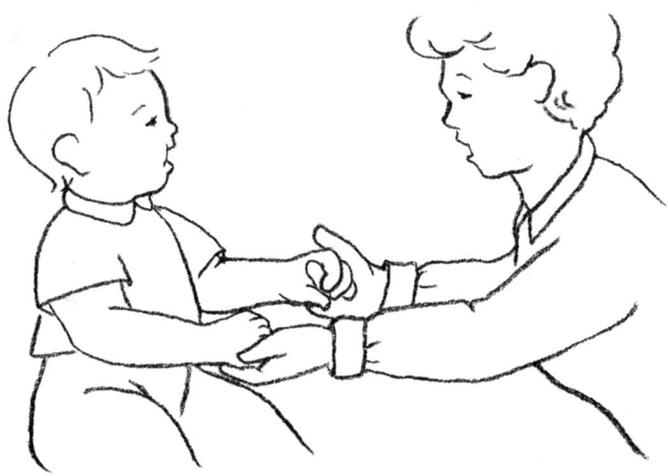

WHAT YOUR BABY WILL LEARN:
Body Awareness

Mirror Parts

- Hold your baby in front of a mirror.
- While he is looking in the mirror, touch his nose and say, "Here's your nose."
- Touch his head and say, "Here's your head."
- Ask the baby to touch his nose. Then ask him to touch his head.
- Touch your nose and say, "Here's my nose." Repeat with your head.
- Ask the baby to touch your nose and head.

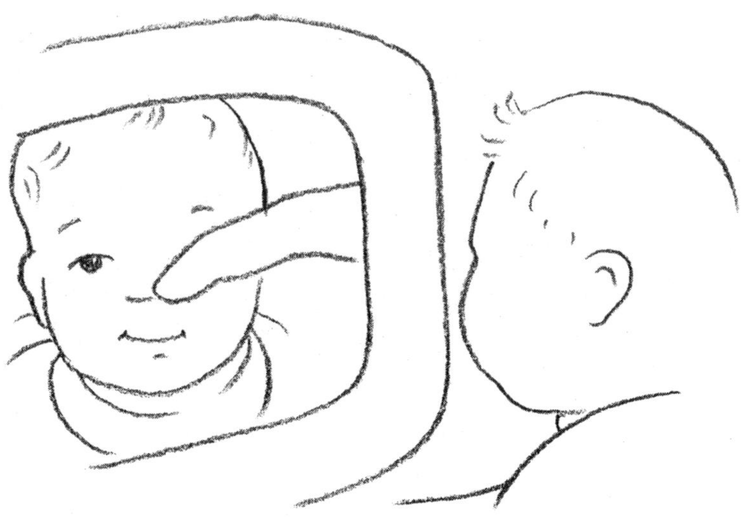

9–12 months

WHAT YOUR BABY WILL LEARN:
Imitation

Open, Shut Them

- (Be prepared for lots of laughter.)
- Your baby will love the surprise ending.
- Recite the poem and act out the words with your fingers as the baby watches.

Open, shut them,
Open, shut them,
Give a little clap.
Open, shut them,
Open, shut them,
Put them in your lap.
Creep them, creep them,
Creep them, creep them,
Right up to your chin.
Open up
Your little mouth,
But do not let them in.

- Start at your waist when you creep to your chin.
- Slow the pace on "Open up your little mouth." Wait a second, then say very quickly, "But do not let them in," and hide your hands behind your back.
- The baby will soon try to imitate your actions.

9–12 months

WHAT YOUR BABY WILL LEARN:
Listening Skills

Copy Me

- Sit on the floor with your baby and gesture for him to copy.

Tap the floor with your hands.
Stick out your tongue and make silly sounds.
Put a hat on your head.
Open and close your fists.
Wiggle your fingers.
Shake your hands.
Shake your head "yes" and "no."
Wave bye-bye.
Make silly sounds with your mouth
Wiggle your index finger over your lips.

- These are only ideas. What is important is talking to your baby while you perform these actions.

9–12 months

WHAT YOUR BABY WILL LEARN:
To Crawl

Tunnel Fun

- Cut off two opposite sides of a large cardboard box.
- Turn the box upside down and encourage your baby to crawl through the tunnel.
- Position a toy at one end of the box and your baby at the other to encourage him to go after the toy. After he has done this once, he will do it over and over.

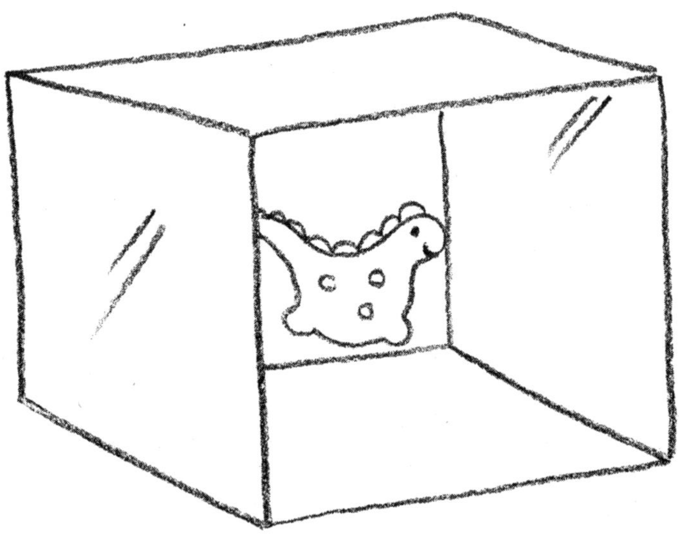

9–12 months

WHAT YOUR BABY WILL LEARN:
To Play Ball

Let's Play Ball

- There are many things that you can do with balls.
- Let your baby explore balls of different sizes and textures.
- Show the baby how to push a ball while crawling on the floor.
- Roll a ball to where your baby is sitting.
- Help your baby roll the ball back to you.
- Show your baby how to hold a ball in the air and let it drop.
- Show the baby how to bounce a ball. As you demonstrate, say, "Bounce, bounce ball."

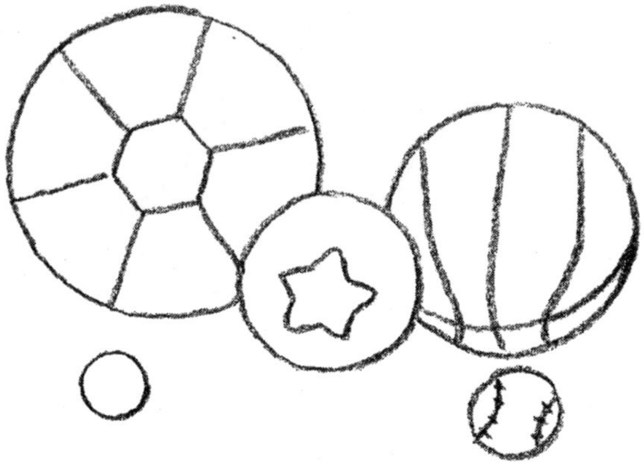

9–12 months

WHAT YOUR BABY WILL LEARN:
Hand-Eye Coordination

The Toy Chase

- Tie a length of string to a small toy that will fit through a toilet paper or paper towel roll. Toys that will roll, like cars, are best for this game. ***NOTE***: Only use toys that are too large for the baby to swallow.
- Make sure the string is longer than the tube.
- Lower the toy into the tube, and then pull it out.
- Hide the toy again, and then tip it out the other end.
- Your baby will delight in this mystery. Say to the disappearing toy, "Bye-bye, toy."
- When the toy reappears, say, "Hello, toy."

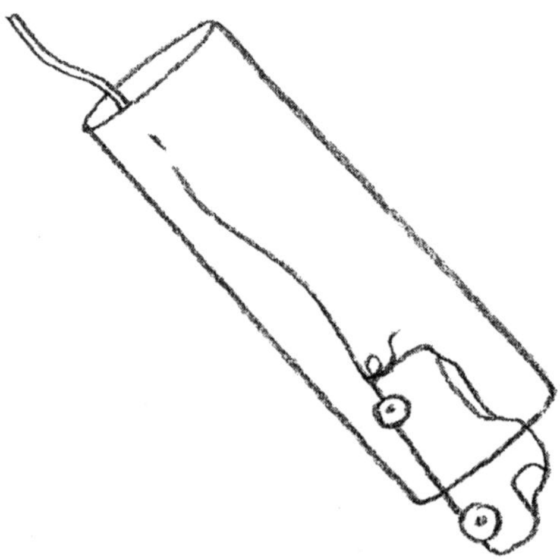

9–12 months

WHAT YOUR BABY WILL LEARN:
Creativity

In the Sky

- Sit on the floor with your baby. Raise his arms out to the side.
- Flap his arms up and down and tell him he is a bird.
- Flap your arms and say, "Tweet, tweet, little bird."
- Flap your baby's arms, saying the same thing.
- Stand up, holding your baby. Stretch one arm outward and pretend that you are an airplane. Make airplane sounds like "zoooom."
- Go outside with your baby and look for birds and airplanes. When you see one, flap your arms and say, "Tweet, tweet" or make airplane sounds.

WHAT YOUR BABY WILL LEARN:
Imagination

Mommy Tunnel

- Stand with your legs spread far enough apart for your baby to fit through them.
- Hold your baby and move him back and forth between your legs.
- Once you have done this a few times, see whether he will crawl or walk through your legs.
- Say, "Here comes the choo-choo train through the tunnel. Choo, choo, choo."
- When he succeeds in going through the "tunnel," praise him a lot.
- Give him a push toy, and see if he will push it through the tunnel.

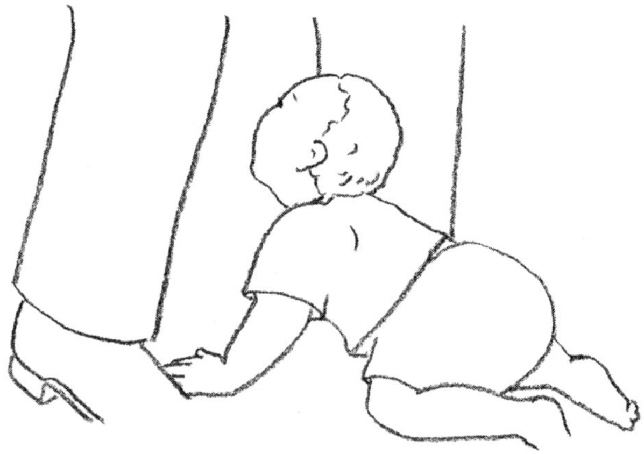

WHAT YOUR BABY WILL LEARN:
Balance

High Steps

- Play this game when your baby is first learning to walk. Balancing is hard, and this game will help him improve his balance.
- Place a few small toys (blocks are good) on the floor.
- Hold the baby's hand as he walks. When he reaches the toys, he will have to lift his foot in order to step over them.
- Show the baby how to march. He will enjoy this, and it is excellent for his muscle development.
- Once the baby can easily step over the blocks, find other blocks, toys, or boxes that are a bit higher. This will be a new challenge for the baby.
- As you both step over the blocks, tell your baby that he is stepping "over" something.
- Also try walking "around" the blocks.

9–12 months

WHAT YOUR BABY WILL LEARN:
Tactile Skills

The Feely-Touchy Game

- Sit on the floor with your baby.
- Put several things with different textures inside a large mixing bowl. If possible, use a metal bowl or cooking pot, because the metal will feel cool to the baby's touch.
- Here are some things that you can put into the bowl:
  - Pieces of cloth with different textures, such as smooth, rough, soft, or furry
  - Sticky piece of tape
  - Bumpy package wrap
- Remove the smooth fabric from the bowl and say, "This is smooth." Give it to your baby and again say, "This is smooth." Ask your baby, "Will you put the smooth cloth back?"
- Continue naming each item in the bowl and then give it to your child. You can also take the item and put it on different parts of your body to see how it feels.
- This game develops the baby's sense of touch as well as his language skills.

WHAT YOUR BABY WILL LEARN:
About Textures

M-m-m Nice

- Put the baby in a sitting position.
- Stock a "feely box" with materials with varied textures, such as a piece of furry material, tissue paper, satin material, or sticky tape. Set the box aside.
- Remove a piece of fur and pat the baby's cheek with it. Rub it along his arms and legs to demonstrate stroking.
- As you stroke the baby with the fur, murmur softly, "M-m-m nice," or "so, so soft," or similar words.
- Give the baby the fur and let him experiment with it.
- Encourage him to pet, stroke, or rub it against him.
- Use tissue paper to demonstrate crushing and foam rubber for squeezing.

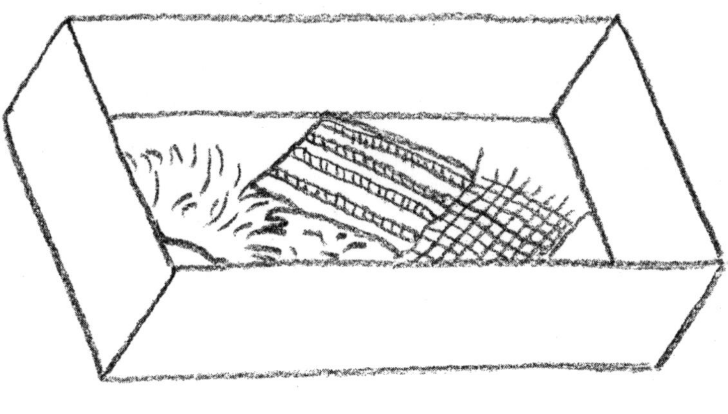

WHAT YOUR BABY WILL LEARN:
Vocabulary

The Bye-bye Game

- Babies at this age are in the "bye-bye" stage. Parents are very proud of their babies when they wave bye-bye.
- When your baby can wave bye-bye, walk around a room and wave to everything.
- Tell the baby, "Wave bye-bye to the chair." Walk to the chair and put his hand on it.
- Then say, "Bye-bye, chair."
- Continue to do this with other objects in the room. You can wave bye-bye to the door, the table, the wall, the doorknob, and so on.
- This not only gives the baby practice in waving, but also helps develop his vocabulary.

WHAT YOUR BABY WILL LEARN:
Creativity

The Banana Game

- Sit your baby in a high chair.
- Put a banana in front of him.
- Pick up the banana and pretend it is a telephone. Say things like "Hello banana, you taste good."
- Ask your baby "Would you like to talk to the banana?"
- Give him the banana and let him pretend to talk on the phone.
- Peel the banana and enjoy eating it together.
- This kind of game stimulates the baby's creativity and originality.

9–12 months

WHAT YOUR BABY WILL LEARN:
Eye-Hand Coordination

The Shoebox Game

- Babies at this age love to put things into containers.
- Shoeboxes are good items to use for this kind of game.
- Cut holes in the lid of a shoebox and find toys that will fit into the holes.
- Film cans are good because babies can easily hold them and push them into the box.
- As your baby succeeds in putting the film cans into the shoebox, praise him and encourage him to do it again.
- This game develops small hand muscles and eye-hand coordination.

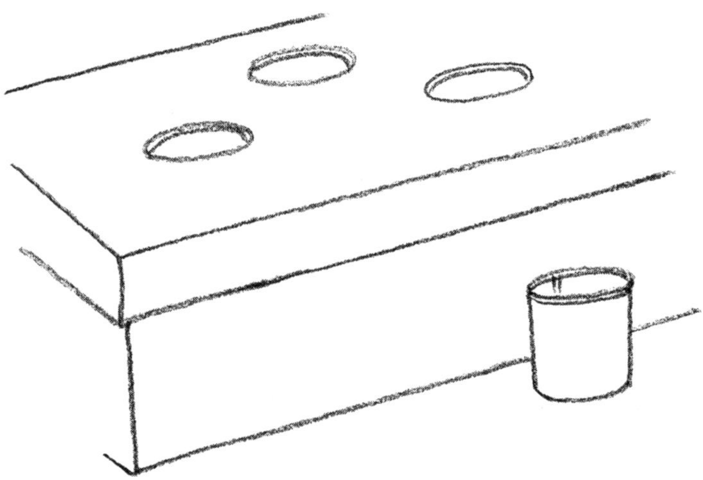

WHAT YOUR BABY WILL LEARN:
Problem-Solving Skills

The Glove Game

- Sit on the floor with your baby.
- Put a garden glove on your hand. Wiggle your fingers inside the glove.
- Put the garden glove on your baby's hand and wiggle the baby's fingers. When you wiggle his fingers, say silly words like "wiggle, wiggle."
- Remove the glove from the baby's hand and see whether he can put it back on by himself. This will probably take time. If he gets frustrated, help and encourage him.
- Play a "glove talk" game with your baby. Put a glove on your baby's hand and one on your hand. Move the glove on your hand and see if he will move the glove on his hand.
- Try putting the glove on the baby's foot.

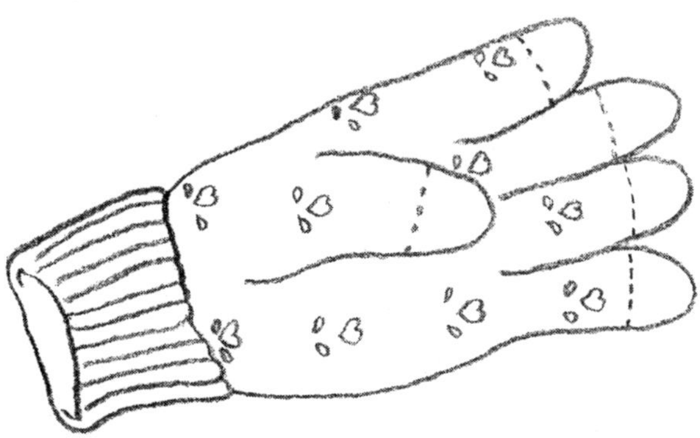

9–12 months

WHAT YOUR BABY WILL LEARN:
Creativity

Two Tube Games

- Pretend that a toilet paper tube or a paper towel tube is a microphone.
- Hold it to your mouth and sing a familiar song.
- Instead of singing through the tube, try making sounds or saying words like your baby does. You might also make announcements through the tube: "Now it's time to play," "Now it's time to eat lunch."
- Cut out two holes from a shoebox lid. (The size of the holes should be the same size as the tubes that you are using.)
- The baby can fit the tubes into the holes and take them out again.

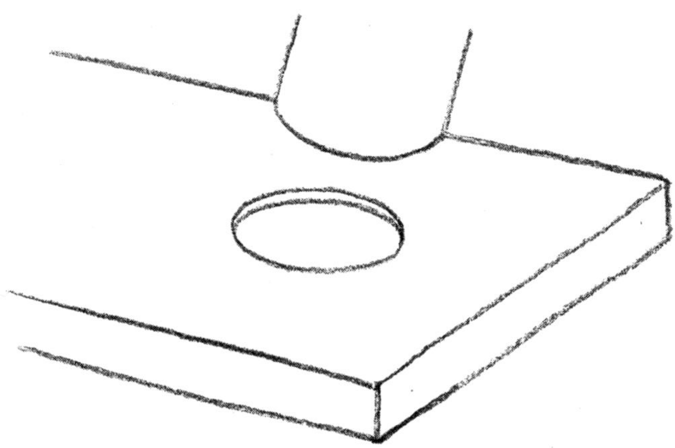

WHAT YOUR BABY WILL LEARN:
To Follow Directions

Upside Down Game

- Turn one of your baby's favorite stuffed animals upside down.
- Next, turn it right side up.
- Turn the toy upside down again. Give it to your baby, and see if he can turn it right side up.
- Recite this rhyme. On the last line—RIGHT SIDE UP!—turn the animal right side up.

Upside down, upside down,
All the world is upside down.
So get ready, here we go,
RIGHT SIDE UP!!

WHAT YOUR BABY WILL LEARN:
Self-Confidence

Sticky Game

- Tape a large piece of contact paper to the floor with the sticky side up.
- Place some of your baby's toys on it.
- Ask him to pull off the toys. He will be amazed at how difficult it is and will feel very proud of himself when he can do it.
- Hold your baby's hands while he walks on the sticky paper. He will have to pull his legs up high in order to get each foot off the paper. Give him constant encouragement.

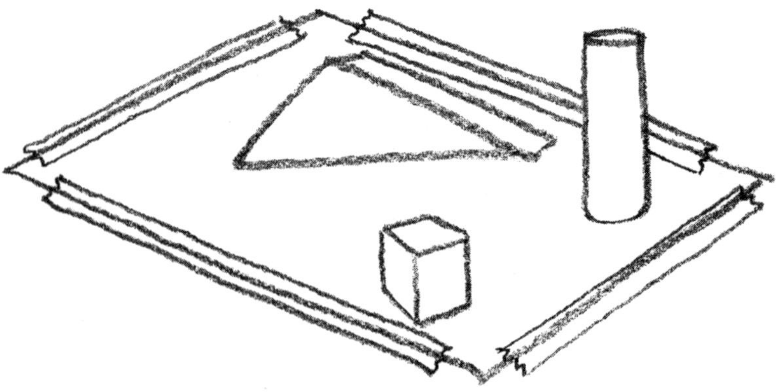

9–12 months

WHAT YOUR BABY WILL LEARN:
Fun

The Cardboard Game

- Collect toy cars and other toys with wheels.
- Fold a large piece of cardboard in half.
- Stand the cardboard up to make a hill for the cars to go down.
- Show your baby how to let the car roll down the cardboard hill.
- Hold a car or toy in your hand and say, "One, two, three, zoom!" Let the car go down the hill.
- See if your baby can learn to wait for the word "zoom" before he releases the car.

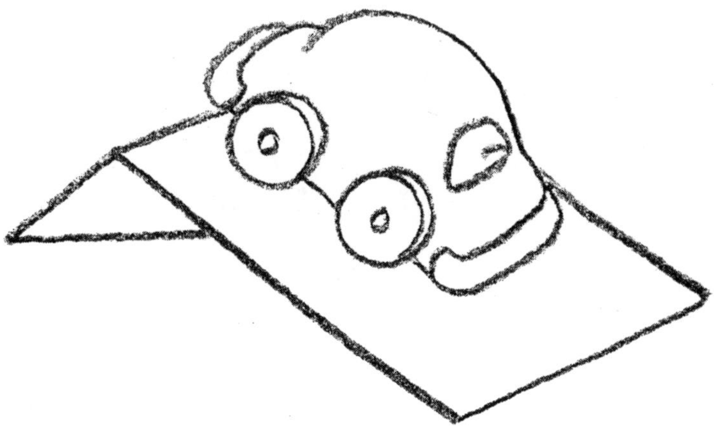

WHAT YOUR BABY WILL LEARN:
Balance

Trampoline Game

- Lie on your back and draw your knees up to your stomach. Cross your feet at the ankles.
- Rest your baby on top of your lower legs. Bounce your legs up and down.
- Move your legs faster and slower as you recite this poem.

> *Bounce, bounce, up and down,*
> *Bounce, bounce all around.*
> *Bounce fast,*
> *Bounce slow,*
> *Bounce, bounce, bounce, bounce, BOOM!*

- On the word "BOOM," lift your baby up and bring him to your chest for a big hug.

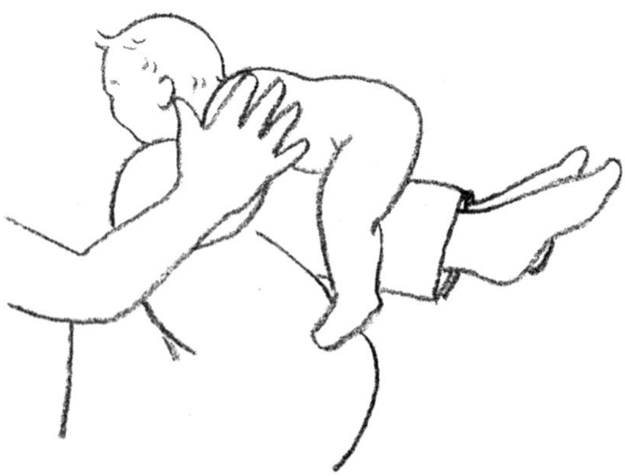

WHAT YOUR BABY WILL LEARN:
Fun

The Elbow Game

- Get your baby's attention. Hold your elbow in front of your face and say, "Where's Daddy?"
- Take your elbow away and say, "Here I am."
- Repeat this several times until the baby begins to try to move your elbow away from your face.
- Hold a stuffed animal or doll and pretend the doll is saying, "Where's Daddy?" This adds another element to the game, making it even more fun.
- Try changing your voice each time you say, "Where's Daddy?"

9–12 months

WHAT YOUR BABY WILL LEARN:
Balance

Pushing Game

- When your baby first learns to walk, he needs lots of practice in balance. Pushing a chair or a stroller can help develop his sense of balance.
- Find a lightweight chair and show the baby how to push it around the house.
- Go outside and let your baby push the stroller.

9–12 months

WHAT YOUR BABY WILL LEARN:
Rhythm

Singing Fun

- Pick three favorite songs that your baby likes to sing. For example, "Twinkle, Twinkle Little Star," "Mary Had a Little Lamb," and "Jingle Bells."
- Clap your hands as you sing one of the songs.
- Put your baby in your lap and sing the song again, clapping the baby's hands.
- Pick a second song, and as you sing, shake bells to the music.
- Sing the second song again, this time letting the baby shake the bells.
- While you sing a third song, hit a wooden spoon against a metal pot.
- Repeat the third song, letting the baby with the spoon.
- Your baby will want to play this game again and again.

9–12 months

WHAT YOUR BABY WILL LEARN:
Listening Skills

Where's the Music?

- Play this game inside or outside. You will need a musical toy or music box.
- Wind up the music box or toy and hide it somewhere in the room or yard.
- Ask the baby, "Where's the music? Let's go find the music."
- Crawl with the baby to a place in the room or yard (for example, to a table). Say to the baby, "Is it here?" Then look and say, "No, it's not here."
- Repeat. On the third try, go to the hiding place and say, "Hooray, we found it!"
- Hide the music box in the same place and repeat the game. Repeat until the baby knows where to go to find the music.
- Next try a new place, and see whether the baby can find it by himself.

9–12 months

WHAT YOUR BABY WILL LEARN:
Language

Speech Rhythms

- The rhythms of speech are pleasing to babies and help them to remember the words they frequently hear.
- Poems and songs play a very important role in this kind of language development.
- Sing songs to your baby. If you sing your favorite songs, he will respond because of your enthusiasm.
- Make up little rhymes about what you are doing. Here are some ideas.

Taking a bath, taking a bath.
Splash, splash
Taking a bath.

Footsie, footsie, where's your footsie?
Yum, yum, kiss your footsie.

Hugs, hugs, I like hugs.
No bugs, just hugs.

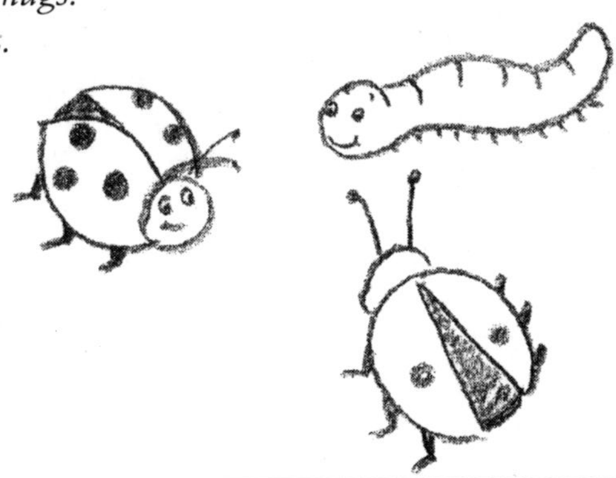

WHAT YOUR BABY WILL LEARN:
Language Skills

Wee Willie Winkie

- This popular and ageless nursery rhyme has charmed generations of children.
- Teach the rhyme to your child and encourage him to say the line "For now it's eight o'clock."

Wee Willie Winkie
Runs through the town,
Upstairs and downstairs
In his nightgown.
Rapping at the windows,
Crying through the locks,
"Are the children in their beds?
For now it's eight o'clock."

WHAT YOUR BABY WILL LEARN:
Language Skills

Huff and Puff

- String a length of twine between the backs of two chairs.
- Fold a large piece of tissue paper in half and hang it over the twine to form a "wall."
- Cut the tissue paper into vertical strips so that the "wolf" can blow its way into the house.
- Tell the story of "The Three Little Pigs."
- When you reach the part where the wolf "huffed and puffed," encourage your child to act out the words.

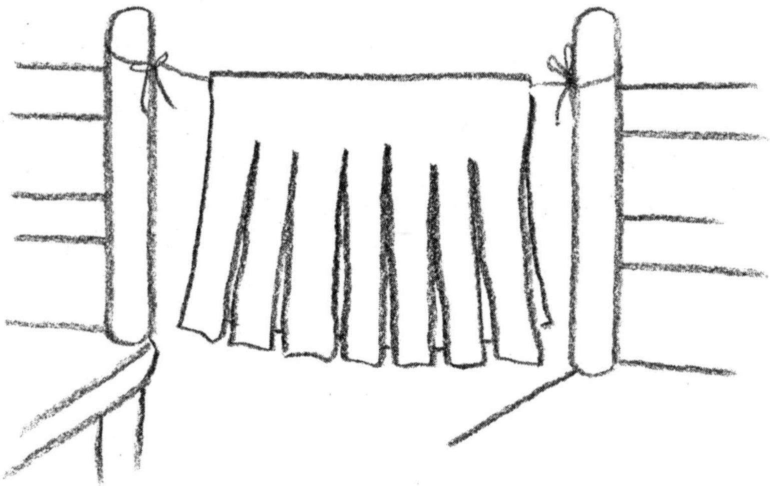

9–12 months

WHAT YOUR BABY WILL LEARN:
Body Awareness

Where's the Foot?

- Draw a picture of a baby on a large piece of heavy paper.
- Glue pieces of material over individual part of the body, such as hands, head, toes, knees and tummy.
- Ask your baby, "Where's the baby's head?" Lift up the material covering the head and say, "Hello, head!"
- Continue this game, naming the other parts.
- Soon your baby will be playing this game by himself.

9–12 months

WHAT YOUR BABY WILL LEARN:
Listening to Directions

Simple Directions

- Babies at this age are learning how to respond to simple directions.
- By practicing how to follow directions, babies develop cognitive thinking.
- Sit on the floor with your baby. Put three toys on the floor next to you.
- Say, "I am going to pick up the ball." Then pick it up.
- Say to your baby, "Can you pick up the ball?" Encourage him to pick up the ball.
- Give the baby another direction, such as "Give the doll a kiss." Give the doll a kiss, and then encourage your baby to do the same.
- Think about the different kinds of directions you can give to your baby. Examples are picking up things, putting down things, and bringing you things.
- Every time your baby succeeds in following directions, he will be very proud of himself.

WHAT YOUR BABY WILL LEARN:
Language Skills

Special Book

- Gather together photographs of family, friends, pets, and anything else with which your baby is familiar.
- Glue each photo on a separate index card. Cover the entire photo with contact paper to protect it.
- Punch a hole at the top left-hand corner of each card and thread string, yarn, or any sturdy cord through all the holes to bind the cards into a book.
- Sit with your baby and talk about each picture. Identify the person and tell the baby something about that person.
- Ask the baby to find a certain picture. "Where's Daddy?" "Where's Aunt Mary?"
- Your baby will delight in seeing so many familiar faces.

Index

Aluminum foil, 156, 158, 197
Animals
pictures, 65
plastic, 174
stuffed, 18, 40, 155, 157, 161, 198, 199, 239, 243
Anticipation games
3 to 6 months, 95–96, 115
6 to 9 months, 122, 160, 175–176
9 to 12 months, 224, 228, 239, 243, 246
Auditory skills
0 to 3 months, 11, 43–44, 46–47, 52–53, 66
3 to 6 months, 11, 79, 83, 104, 106–107, 110
6 to 9 months, 12–13, 152, 156, 162–163, 173, 176
9 to 12 months, 12–13, 216, 219, 225, 245–246, 251
Baby oil, 134
Balancing skills
3 to 6 months, 92
6 to 9 months, 164
9 to 12 months, 214, 222, 231, 242, 244
Balls, 58, 140, 147, 227, 251
beach, 138
Bananas, 194, 206, 235
Baskets, 142
Bath activities
0 to 3 months, 34
3 to 6 months, 73, 83
6 to 9 months, 125
9 to 12 months, 187–192
Bathtubs, 73, 83, 125, 187-192
Beach balls, 138
Bedtime/crib activities
0 to 3 months, 18–21, 51, 60
3 to 6 months, 71–72
6 to 9 months, 134, 136, 170
9 to 12 months, 179–183, 248
Bells, 52, 58, 82, 106, 216, 245
Blankets, 18, 26, 35, 137, 159
Blocks, 117, 146, 147, 171, 213, 231
Body awareness
0 to 3 months, 22, 27, 30–32, 38, 45, 63
3 to 6 months, 71, 76, 78, 80, 82, 84–88, 97, 104
6 to 9 months, 128–130
9 to 12 months, 186, 188, 217, 220–223, 250
Books
baby, 168
photo, 252
roly-poly, 118
Bottles
covers, 101
plastic, 187, 214
baby, 19, 23, 101, 121
Bowls, 98
metal, 232
plastic, 74, 208
Boxes, 103, 198, 213, 226, 231, 233
cereal, 214
lids, 213, 236, 238
oatmeal, 118
shoe, 236
Bubble wrap, 232
Buckets, 204
Buttons, 211
Cans
juice, 214
coffee, 140, 215
Cardboard, 65, 158, 241
tubes, 228, 238
Carpet, 157, 159
Cars, 196
toy, 215, 241
CD players, 162, 173, 176
Cereal, 99, 206-207, 209-210
Chairs, 48, 52, 141, 145, 200, 234, 244, 249
high, 99, 104, 146-148, 150, 154, 171, 205-206, 235
Chants. *See* Rhymes
Clothespins, 213, 215
Coffee cans, 140, 215
Cognitive skills
0 to 3 months, 11–12, 53, 56, 58, 64–65
3 to 6 months, 11–12, 75, 116–117
6 to 9 months, 13, 124, 133, 153, 160, 167, 175
9 to 12 months, 13, 185, 189, 199–202, 209, 211–213, 216, 218, 228, 237
Colors
0 to 3 months, 56, 58, 64–65
3 to 6 months, 81
9 to 12 months, 216
black and white, 56
bright, 25, 36, 84
gloves, 84
socks, 64, 84, 85
toys, 90
Combs, 185
Contact paper, 118, 216, 240, 252
Containers
margarine, 214
plastic, 106, 205
Cooking activities, 74
Coordination
0 to 3 months, 33, 55, 62
3 to 6 months, 77, 82, 88–89, 92, 98–100, 102, 104
6 to 9 months, 123, 128, 140–142, 144, 146, 148–152, 154, 171–182

9 to 12 months, 190–192, 197, 205–210, 214–215, 219–220, 227–228, 231–232, 236–238, 241–242, 244
Cotton balls, 26, 158
Counting activities, 211
Crackers, 149, 205, 209
Crawling activities
6 to 9 months, 140–141, 145, 159
9 to 12 months, 226, 230
Creativity
6 to 9 months, 150
9 to 12 months, 197–198, 210, 213, 217–218, 229–230, 235, 238, 249
Cups
measuring, 212
paper, 207
plastic, 148, 154, 192, 208
Diapers, 144
changing activities, 22, 27, 52, 80, 126–127, 186
cloth, 94
Dolls, 147, 155, 161, 185, 243, 251
Drinking straws, 154
Dropping games, 140, 146, 156, 171, 204, 213, 215, 227
Eggs
cartons, 214
plastic, 106
Emery boards, 158
Fabrics
burlap, 103
corduroy, 158
flannel, 29
linen, 29
satin, 158, 233
silk, 26, 29, 101, 123, 144, 159, 201, 232, 250
velvet, 29, 103, 158, 159
Film canisters, 106, 149, 236
Fine motor skills
0 to 3 months, 33, 45, 62
3 to 6 months, 74, 77, 98–100, 102, 104, 106–107
6 to 9 months, 123–124, 140, 142, 146, 148–152, 154, 171–172
9 to 12 months, 190–192, 197, 206–209, 214–215, 219, 236–238, 241
Fingerplays, 220–221, 224
"Where Is Thumbkin?" 88
Finger puppets, 68
Flashlights, 67
Floating toys, 189, 191
Foil
aluminum, 156, 158, 197
pie pans, 46, 172
Foods, 98–101, 149–150, 153, 194, 205–210
Fruits
bananas, 194, 206, 235
melons, 194
raisins, 210
Fur, 103, 233
Games
Body, 114
Bye-Bye, 234
Choo Choo, 164
Cockle Doodle Doo, 97
Dropping, 140, 146, 156, 171, 204, 213, 215, 227
Floating, 144
Here Comes the Bug, 96
Hide-and-Seek, 145, 200–203, 209, 246
Name, 113
Outdoor, 145
Peek-a-Boo, 94, 122–123, 189, 193, 243, 250
Spider, 95
Tug-of-War, 143
Where's the Mousie? 135
Where's Your Toe? 129
Gloves, 29
garden, 237
sock, 84
Glue, 65, 158, 250, 252
Grass, 35, 145
Guidelines for growth
0 to 6 months, 11–12
6 to 12 months, 12–13
Gym mats, 139
Hats, 113, 217
Hide-and-seek games, 145, 200–203, 209, 246
High chairs, 99, 104, 146-148, 150, 154, 171, 205-206, 235
Ice, 208
Index cards, 252
Infant seats, 74, 122
Jars, 149, 205
Jell-O, 100
Juice cans, 214
Language skills
0 to 3 months, 11–12, 25, 36–37, 39–41, 50–52, 54–55, 57
3 to 6 months, 11–12, 73–75, 78, 84–86, 89–90, 92–93, 104–105, 108–109, 111–115, 118
6 to 9 months, 13, 124–126, 129, 131, 136–139, 141–143, 147, 157–160, 164–170, 174–176
9 to 12 months, 13, 180–183, 184, 188, 194–196, 199, 202, 204–206, 210–213, 217–218, 221–223, 225–226, 232, 234, 239, 242, 247–252
Large motor skills
0 to 3 months, 36–37, 39–41, 52, 57
3 to 6 months, 89–90, 92–93
6 to 9 months, 125, 136–139, 141, 143, 159
9 to 12 months, 204–205, 210, 212–213, 218, 222, 226–226, 240, 242
Laundry baskets, 142
Leaves, 204
Lids, 106, 149
box, 213
cup, 154

pan, 153
shoebox, 236, 238
Lights, 20
switches, 160
Macaroni, 150
Magazines, 56, 118, 168
Marbles, 106
Margarine containers, 214
Markers, 56, 84
Meal time activities
3 to 6 months, 98–101, 104
6 to 9 months, 121, 148–150, 154
9 to 12 months, 205–207, 209–210, 235
Measuring cups, 212
Memory
3 to 6 months, 117
9 to 12 months, 199–202, 209, 216
Milk cartons, 210, 214, 215, 216
Mirrors, 57, 59, 161, 217, 223
Mittens, 218
Mobiles, 58
Motor skills
0 to 3 months, 11, 33, 36–37, 39–41, 62
3 to 6 months, 11, 73, 77, 89–90, 92–93, 98–100, 102, 106–107
6 to 9 months, 12–13, 124–125, 137–143, 146, 148–152, 154, 159, 171–172
9 to 12 months, 12–13, 190–192, 197, 204–210, 212–215, 218–219, 222, 226–227, 230–231, 236–238, 240–242, 244
fine, 33, 45, 62, 74, 77, 98–100, 102, 104, 106–107, 123–124, 140, 142, 146, 148–152, 154, 171–172, 190–192, 197, 206–209, 214–215, 219, 236–238, 241
large, 36–37, 39–41, 52, 57, 89–90, 92–93, 125, 136–139, 141, 143, 159, 204–205, 210, 212–213, 218, 222, 226–227, 240, 242
Mozart, Wolfgang Amadeus, 53
Muffin tins, 151
Music
classical, 53, 133, 162, 173
boxes, 246
instrumental, 176
vocal, 176
marches, 173
ballet, 173
Music appreciation games
0 to 3 months, 53
3 to 6 months, 104
6 to 9 months, 133, 162, 172–173, 176
9 to 12 months, 219, 245–246
Napkins, 123
Newspaper, 152
Nursery Rhymes, 105
"Baa, Baa, Black Sheep," 39
"Diddle, Diddle, Dumpling," 39
Object permanence. *See* Peek-a-boo games
Opposites, 75
Outdoor activities
0 to 3 months, 33
6 to 9 months, 145
9 to 12 months, 196, 204, 218, 229
Pans, 153
pie, 46, 172
Paper towel tubes, 228, 238
Paper, 156, 250
cups, 207
Patterns, 56, 65
Peek-a-boo games, 94, 122–123, 189, 193, 243, 250
Photographs, 165, 252
Pictures, 56, 65, 118, 126–127, 168, 250
Pie pans, 46, 172
Pillows, 40, 57, 141
Plastic
animals, 174
bottles, 187, 214
bowls, 74, 208
containers, 106, 205
cups, 148, 208
eggs, 106
glasses, 209
spoons, 74
Play activities
0 to 3 months, 28
3 to 6 months, 79, 83, 94–96
6 to 9 months, 123, 127–128, 132, 135, 151, 155
9 to 12 months, 184, 187, 227, 241, 243
Poems. *See* Rhymes
Poster board, 56
Pots, 153, 232, 245
Pre-math skills, 211–212
Pre-reading skills
3 to 6 months, 105, 118
6 to 9 months, 168
9 to 12 months, 252
Problem-solving games, 153, 216, 237
Pull toys, 198, 203, 210
Puppets
finger, 68
Push toys, 230, 244
Raisins, 210
Rattles, 30, 33, 43, 52, 107, 113, 128, 171
homemade, 106
Refrigerators, 157, 195
Rhymes, 47, 71, 105, 247
"Bounce, Bounce, Boom!" 242
"Bouncy, Bouncy Baby," 92
"Copy Me," 225
"Creeping, Creeping, Creeping," 131
"Fingers and Toes," 84
"Five Little Fingers," 85
"I See the Moon," 183
"Jelly in the Bowl," 100
"Little Mouse," 132
"Mr. Bear," 199
"One Button," 211
"One, Two, Kick," 137
"Open, Shut Them," 224
"Pinkety Pinkety," 130
"Powder Puff," 186

"Right Side Up!" 239
"Roll the Ball," 138
"Shoe the Old Horse," 184
"Stretch Up High," 136
"Swim Little Fishy," 73
"Tap and Clap," 219
"This Little Pig," 31
"This Little Piggy," 87
"This Little Toe," 83
"Through the Hole," 220
"Wee Willie Winkie," 248
"Where, Oh Where?" 32
"Whoops, Johnny," 221
"Zip, Zip, Zip," 127
Ribbon, 155, 203
Rolling over, 41, 91
Safety skills, 196
Satin, 158, 233
Scarves, 102, 144, 157, 159, 201
Self-concept skills
0 to 3 months, 12, 49
3 to 6 months, 12, 122
6 to 9 months, 13–14, 168
9 to 12 months, 13–14, 205, 240
Shakers, 106
Shapes
0 to 3 months, 56, 58, 65
6 to 9 months, 133
9 to 12 months, 218
Shirts, 166, 211
Shoeboxes, 236
Shoes, 166, 184
Sign language, 167
Singing activities, 34, 42, 52, 89, 134, 238, 247
Sitting up, 222
Social skills
0 to 3 months, 25, 27, 49
3 to 6 months, 108, 111–1126 to 9 months, 143, 169
9 to 12 months, 185, 203, 224–225, 234, 239, 251
Socks 64, 84-85, 101, 143, 166
Songs
"All the Pretty Horses," 21
"Brahm's Lullaby," 170
"Farmer in the Dell," 171
"Go 'Round and 'Round the Mountain," 38
"Good Night, Baby," 179
"Hush Little Baby," 21, 170
"Hush-a-bye," 21, 72, 170
"It's Raining, It's Pouring," 187
"Jingle Bells," 245
"Mary Had a Little Lamb," 47, 171, 172, 175, 245
"Newcastle Lullaby," 181
"Niño Querido," 180
"Old MacDonald," 174-175
"Rain, Rain, Go Away," 187
"Rock-a-Bye Baby," 21
"Row, Row, Row Your Boat," 109, 172
"Twinkle, Twinkle, Little Star," 19, 47, 110, 175, 245
"Where Is Thumbkin?" 88
Sousa, John Phillip, 173
Spatial relationships, 199, 212
Spoons, 98, 152, 172, 205, 208, 219
measuring, 74
metal, 152
wooden, 74, 104, 152, 245
Squeaky toys, 40, 45
Squeeze toys, 190
Stories, 182
"Three Little Pigs," 249
String, 65, 198, 228, 252
Strollers, 244
Stuffed animals, 18, 40, 155, 157, 161, 198-199, 239, 243
Swan Lake, 173
Swimming pools, 73
Swings, 74
Tables, 141, 152, 234
Tactile awareness games
0 to 3 months, 17, 19, 23, 26, 28–29, 35, 62–63
3 to 6 months, 76, 100–101, 103
6 to 9 months, 132, 134–135, 144–145, 156–159
9 to 12 months, 186–187, 190, 194–195, 197, 204, 227, 232–233, 240
Tape players, 162, 173, 176
Tape, 56, 103, 216, 232-233, 240
Teethers, 33
Telephones, 163
banana, 235
toy, 169
Televisions, 163
Texture board, 158
Tissue paper, 156, 197, 233, 249
Toilet paper tubes, 228, 238
Towels, 188
Trust/bonding activities
0 to 3 months, 17–21, 23–24, 26, 34, 42
3 to 6 months, 71–72, 76, 78, 87, 91, 93
6 to 9 months, 121–122, 129–130, 134, 170
9 to 12 months, 179–181, 193
Twine, 249
Umbrellas, 58
Vegetables, 99
Velvet, 103, 158, 159
Visual skills
0 to 3 months, 11, 48, 56–61, 64–65, 67–68
3 to 6 months, 11, 81, 116
6 to 9 months, 12–13, 126, 161
9 to 12 months, 12–13, 204
Walking exercises, 231, 240, 244
Washcloths, 188-191
Water, 73, 83, 125, 163, 187–192, 207–208
Wax paper, 158
Wooden spoons, 104, 152, 245
Wrapping paper, 156
Yarn, 82, 210, 252